The New Business Incubator

The New Business Incubator

Linking Talent, Technology, Capital, and Know-How

Raymond W. Smilor
Michael Doud Gill, Jr.
IC^2 Institute
The University of Texas at Austin

Lexington Books
D.C. Heath and Company/Lexington, Massachusetts/Toronto

Library of Congress Cataloging-in-Publication Data

Smilor, Raymond W.
  The new business incubator.

  Bibliography: p.
  Includes index.
  1. New business enterprises.   2. Entrepreneur.
I. Gill, Michael D.   II. Title.
HD62.5.S624   1986   658.1′1   85-45009
ISBN 0-669-11096-5 (alk. paper)

Published simultaneously in Canada
Printed in the United States of America
Casebound International Standard Book Number: 0-669-11096-5
Library of Congress Catalog Card Number: 85-45009

The paper used in this publication meets the minimum requirements of American National Standard for Information Sciences—Permanence of Paper for Printed Library Materials, ANSI Z39.48-1984.   ∞™

ISBN 0-669-11096-5

86 87 88 89 90 8 7 6 5 4 3 2 1

To Ronya and George Kozmetsky,
with appreciation for their
remarkable incubating abilities

Contents

Figures and Tables

Figures

Tables

Preface

Three key assumptions are the drivers for this book. First, we are on the threshold of a great entrepreneurial era. Not only in the United States but across the world, more attention is being focused on the entrepreneurial phenomenon—the rapid increase in and the diversity of new business ventures.

Second, the environment for new business development is intensely, indeed fiercely, competitive. It is, in fact, hypercompetitive. The competition is likely to increase, not decrease. How communities, regions, and nations anticipate and respond to this competition will largely determine the health and viability of their economies.

Third, because of the dynamics of entrepreneurship and the thrust of hypercompetition, the nature of economic development has fundamentally changed. New institutional developments are altering the tactics and strategies of economic development and diversification. New relationships between the public and private sectors—especially among business, government, and academia—are having profound consequences on the way we think about and take action on economic development.

The concept of the new business incubator is related to all three of these assumptions. It seeks to leverage entrepreneurial talent, respond to a hypercompetitive environment, and implement new institutional relationships for innovative economic development.

However, because the concept is new, even experimental, there has been little hard data or clear evidence on the success of incubators. Fortunately, more research is being undertaken on the incubator concept.

This book seeks to shed light on how well incubators are leveraging entrepreneurial talent, how effectively they are responding to a hypercompetitive environment, and to what degree they are proving to be a successful economic development mechanism.

Acknowledgments

Many entrepreneurial people and organizations helped nurture the development of this book.

We are grateful to Dr. George Kozmetsky, director of the IC² Institute at The University of Texas at Austin, for his support, encouragement, and insightful critique.

F. Selby Clark provided valuable research assistance. Many of the figures that appear in this book are the result of his skill on the Macintosh. In addition, his primary research contributed significantly to the case studies of the Fulton-Carroll Center and to Technology Centers International.

Dr. Robert Peterson, the Charles Hurwitz Centennial Fellow in the IC² Institute, was extremely helpful in developing the incubator survey document.

Three organizations gave invaluable support to the study reported here. The IC² Institute at The University of Texas at Austin gave us the time and administrative support to work on the project. This research effort reflects the Institute's commitment to entrepreneurial research and to a better understanding of new institutional developments. We greatly appreciate the many contributions of the IC² staff: Elaine Chamberlain, Ophelia Mallari, Linda Teague, and Becky Younger.

The U.S. Small Business Administration's Office of Private Sector Initiatives played a key role in initiating the project. The funding that it provided for this study demonstrates its concern for a better understanding of the concept of the new business incubator. We wish to thank John Cox, director of the Office of Private Sector Initiatives; Jeff Weiss, deputy district director of the Washington district office; and Samantha Silva, business development specialist in the San Francisco district office, for their support and encouragement.

Peat, Marwick, Mitchell & Co. provided an important grant to conduct the national survey. We especially appreciate the support and confidence of S. Thomas Moser, national director of Peat Marwick's High Technology Practice.

We were very fortunate to have the IC² Institute, the Office of Private Sector Initiatives, and Peat, Marwick as sponsors of the study because they left the development of the survey, the analysis of the data, and the reporting of the results entirely to us.

We are particularly grateful to a number of key individuals who so generously shared not only their time but especially their insights and experience on the incubator concept:

Dr. Wayne Brown, founder and former chairman, the Utah Innovation Center, Salt Lake City, Utah.

Bradley Bertoch, executive director, and Gregg Goodwin, program administrator, the Utah Innovation Foundation, Salt Lake City, Utah.

Dr. Stephen Szygenda and J. Jette Campbell, cofounders, and George Pearson, president, The Rubicon Group, Austin, Texas.

June Lavelle, executive director, Fulton-Carroll Center for Industry, Chicago, Illinois.

Loren Schultz, president, Technology Centers International, Inc., Montgomeryville, Pennsylvania.

Eric Siegel, acting manager, Paoli Technology Enterprise Center, Paoli, Pennsylvania.

Jean Vandergrift, general manager, Lansdale Technology Enterprise Center, Lansdale, Pennsylvania.

Ben Hill, manager of business development, and Don Plumber, director of information, Advanced Technology Development Center, Georgia Institute of Technology, Atlanta, Georgia.

Jerome Mahone, director, Rensselaer Polytechnic Institute Incubator, Troy, New York.

James Greenwood, director of economic development, Los Alamos Economic Development Corporation, Los Alamos, New Mexico.

Jeffrey Nathanson, executive director, New Mexico Business Innovation Center, Albuquerque, New Mexico.

John Thorne, president, Enterprise Corporation of Pittsburgh, Pittsburgh, Pennsylvania;

Sharon O'Flanagan, national sales manager, Control Data Business and Technology Centers, Minneapolis, Minnesota.

Michael D. Newman, manager, Control Data Business and Technology Center, Minneapolis, Minnesota.

Robert McKinley, director, Control Data Business and Technology Center, San Antonio, Texas.

We benefited from discussions with

Dr. Eugene Stark, chairman, Federal Laboratory Consortium, Los Alamos, New Mexico.

Dr. Christopher W. LeMaistre, director, Center for Industrial Innovation, Rensselaer Polytechnic Institute, Troy, New York.

Dr. Peter Zandan, associate editor, *Journal of High Technology Marketing*, Austin, Texas.

The Honorable George Busbee, former governor, State of Georgia.

Dr. Terry K. Dorsey, president, United Capital Ventures, Inc.

Dr. Thomas Steltson, vice-president for research, Georgia Institute of Technology.

Robert Hutton, president, Technology Fund, Montgomeryville, Pennsylvania.

We also learned from the research of David N. Allen, assistant professor in the Institute of Public Administration, The Pennsylvania State University, and Candace Campbell, executive director of the Minnesota Center for Community Economic Development.

Caroline McCarley at Lexington Books is a great editor with whom to work. She has a real talent for combining patience with persistence. Her sharp eye improved the manuscript. Karen E. Maloney of Lexington provided important assistance as production editor for the book.

Special thanks go to Judy Smilor, an entrepreneurial partner in the adventure of incubating two promising fledglings, Matthew and Kevin. Without their support and especially the time they provided, this book would not yet have "hatched."

Engracia Gill deserves special thanks for providing invaluable support, encouragement and love throughout the entire challenging process to one of the co-authors.

We appreciate the contributions of everyone who helped with this book. Yet we want to emphasize that the conclusions are our own and that any errors are ours alone.

Our hope is that this book contributes not only to a better understanding of the incubator concept but also to a more effective implementation of the idea.

The New Business
Incubator

1
Introduction

The word *incubate* takes on fascinating connotations when it is applied to new business development. To incubate means to maintain under prescribed and controlled conditions an environment favorable for hatching or developing. It also means to cause to develop or to give form and substance to something. In this context, an incubator is an apparatus for the maintenance of controlled conditions for cultivation.

To incubate fledgling companies implies an ability or desire to maintain some kinds of prescribed and controlled conditions favorable to the development of new firms. The incubator seeks to give form and substance—that is, structure and credibility—to start-up or emerging ventures. Consequently, a new business incubator is a facility for the maintenance of controlled conditions to assist in the cultivation of new companies.

The controlled conditions include four types of resources: secretarial support, administrative assistance, facilities support, and business expertise, including management, marketing, accounting, and finance. By controlling these conditions, the business incubator seeks to effectively link talent, technology, capital, and know-how in order to leverage entrepreneurial talent and to accelerate the development of new companies.

The Growth of Incubators

The process of "hatching" new businesses, of incubating emerging enterprises, seeks to speed company growth and to provide an innovative approach to economic development. The new business incubator, consequently, is attracting widespread attention in the United States and in many other countries, including France, Germany, Sweden, England, Japan, and China. It goes under a variety of names including "innovation center," "enterprise center," and "business and technology center."

The number of incubators in the United States has grown rapidly in recent years. As shown in figure 1–1, 89.3 percent of the incubators responding

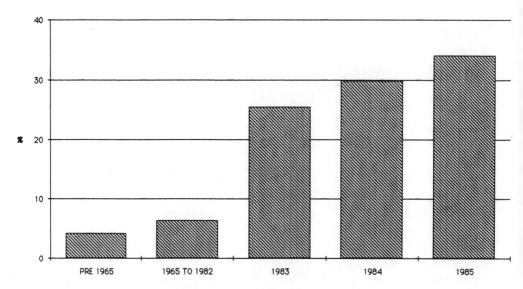

Figure 1–1. Year Incubator Opened

to our national survey whose results are reported in chapters 5 and 6 have been opened since 1983—and 34 percent were opened in 1985 alone. There are now approximately 150 incubators operating or being planned in the United States.

These incubators are widely dispersed geographically in the United States. As shown in table 1–1, incubators have emerged in every region of the country. Some experts predict the number will double in the next year.

The Small Business Administration's Office of Private Sector Initiatives has conducted national conferences on the incubator idea with a variety of public and private sector cosponsors. It has also started a nationally distributed newsletter, *Incubator Times*. Incubator development companies have emerged to help set up incubators, and a national organization has been formed to address incubator issues. The National Business Incubation Association, a nonprofit association headquartered in Alexandria, Virginia, was established in 1985. It seeks to promote business incubators, inform and educate others about the benefits of incubators, provide information on incubator development, monitor legislation, and bring together key individuals involved in the business incubator "industry."

The concept has generated great enthusiasm. An economic development publication called it "the most potent economic development tool to be introduced in this decade."[1] It has also caused skepticism. A February 1986 article in *Venture* magazine wondered if tenant companies might not be giving up far more than they are getting by being in an incubator.[2]

Table 1–1
Survey Respondents, by State

State	Incubators Responding to Survey	Total Number of Incubators in State	Percent Responding
California	3	14	21
Colorado	1	1	100
Connecticut	1	2	50
Georgia	0	1	0
Illinois	2	7	29
Indiana	0	2	0
Iowa	1	1	100
Maryland	1	2	50
Massachusetts	1	3	33
Michigan	6	9	67
Minnesota	2	9	22
Mississippi	0	1	0
Missouri	0	2	0
Nebraska	0	1	0
New Jersey	1	1	100
New York	5	7	71
Ohio	6	8	75
Oklahoma	2	4	50
Oregon	0	1	0
Pennsylvania	9	25	36
Rhode Island	1	1	100
South Carolina	0	4	0
Tennessee	2	2	100
Texas	1	2	50
Utah	1	1	100
Vermont	1	2	50
Washington	2	3	67
Wisconsin	1	1	100
Total (28 states)	50	117	43

Two Broad Strategies

As the concept began to evolve in the early 1980s, two broad strategies emerged. Both strategies could be appropriate and effective for the location and purpose of an incubator. One approach was to renovate older or vacant buildings, such as schools, factories, or warehouses, and lease space at relatively inexpensive rates. The strategy focused more on providing entrepreneurs with access to space than on building companies—that is, on expanding operations, personnel, and markets. Success was defined in terms of lease space and in terms of the entrepreneur's ability to meet monthly expenses.

The second strategy was a more conscious attempt to build companies— that is, to leverage resources to help companies grow. With this strategy, some incubators sought an equity position in tenant companies. Although providing space was still important, the focus was on developing firms. Success was defined in terms of tenant company expansion and ability to eventually stand on its own.

As the incubator concept has developed, there has been an increasing emphasis on the second strategy—helping companies to grow. And incubators have been experimenting with a variety of tactics to link talent, technology, capital, and know-how.

To appreciate business incubator development, it is important to realize that the idea is relatively new. It is still an experiment, and as with all experiments, a great deal of testing is taking place.

Examples of Incubators

The testing of the incubator concept is reflected in the diversity of incubator organizations.[3]

Rensselaer Polytechnic Institute (RPI), a Troy, New York, university, started its incubator in 1980. Rensselaer provides entrepreneurial firms inexpensive space for operations and access to campus facilities. Transactions are on a cash basis, although RPI has accepted stock in a company as payment for rent. In a related development, the New York state legislature has established the New York Center for Industrial Innovation at RPI. The center has both public and private sector support. As a research facility, the center provides an additional resource that may assist the incubator's development.

The **Advanced Technology Development Center** (ATDC) at the Georgia Institute of Technology in Atlanta is a state-sponsored program that runs an integrated program of incubation and entrepreneurial stimulation and assistance. Started in 1980, the ATDC has a consulting arm and incubation space. Its consulting division, the Georgia Advanced Technology Development Corporation, has a permanent staff and a number of technical consultants. The ATDC supports tenant companies for no longer than three years, after which it either helps them obtain other financing sources or uses its venture capital subsidiary to fund them. The ATDC screens applications from prospective entrepreneurs, grooms their business plans and presentations, and then brings in venture capitalists to review their proposals.

The **Utah Innovation Center** (UIC), in Salt Lake City, is a private incubation facility that developed from a quasi-public organization affiliated with the University of Utah. Started in 1978 with a grant from the National Science Foundation Innovation Center Program, the UIC is privately funded by individuals. Dr. Wayne Brown, the founder of the UIC and its principal owner, is a former dean of the College of Engineering at the University of Utah. He is a successful entrepreneur himself and is the guiding force behind the incubator concept in Utah. UIC operations are funded from the center's capitalization and from income from continuing operations. For cash flow, the center consults with nonincubator firms, forms R&D partnerships to carry out research at the center, leases office space in UIC buildings, and applies for government grants. The UIC takes up to a one-third equity position in firms located within its center. In return, the UIC provides all services commonly associated with incubators.

Technology Centers International (TCI), started in 1976 in Montgomeryville, Pennsylvania, was one of the nation's first incubators. Since its first incubation center—or Technology Enterprise Center (TEC)—was opened, other centers have been opened in other regions of the country. Besides the usual range of support services, the TECs also offer consulting services. Each TEC has a "Center Champion," who is responsible for helping the tenants develop business plans, marketing strategies, and financing opportunities. The position of Champion is designed for an experienced entrepreneur with a variety of personal contacts.

Each Technology Enterprise Center seeks to develop a pool of capital for funding potential tenants and for participating in a national fund, the Technology Fund. The idea is that the local pool of capital should be financed primarily with local and regional capital; it is designated to provide start-up or seed funding for small companies. Each local fund is also supposed to help capitalize a national fund, which invests in follow-on financing for outstanding companies supported by local funds.

The **Rubicon Group** is located in Austin, Texas. It has a panel of advisers, each with distinct expertise in the financial, marketing, legal, or technological areas. Rubicon funds tenant companies through a pool of capital that is set up as a partnership. Each investment is established as a joint venture between the entrepreneur and the Rubicon Group's investment partnership. Rubicon typically retains a majority percentage of a company's equity for its investment and services and plans a two-year turnover of all its companies. Within the two-year period, each tenant firm will either fail, grow large enough to make it on its own, or expand outside the incubator with follow-on financing.

The **Fulton-Carroll Center for Industry** in Chicago, Illinois, is a renovated 1891 factory building. The incubator operates in an urban renewal area under the leadership of its executive director, June Lavelle. It opened in 1980 when the Industrial Council of Northwest Chicago, a private, not-for-profit organization, received a $1.7 million federal grant to buy and renovate the building. The center has a flexible admission policy (it does not require a detailed business plan), accepts a wide variety of companies (not just high-tech), and provides a range of services from secretarial support to loading docks. Of the fifty-three businesses that have rented space, fourteen have graduated, five have failed, and thirty-four remain. Of the 317 employees within tenant firms, 76 percent are from a 3-mile radius, and most are minorities.[4]

The **Los Alamos Economic Development Corporation** was established in 1985 as a private, nonprofit organization. After $280,000 had been spent to renovate a building, the incubator was fully occupied within a few months. The incubator is informally associated with Los Alamos National Laboratory, with the aim of helping to commercialize federally funded research. A number of the tenant companies are, indeed, spin-offs from the national lab. The incubator provides shared services, access to consulting expertise and financial resources, and a supportive climate for start-ups.

The **Enterprise Corporation of Pittsburgh,** Pennsylvania, is a private, nonprofit corporation affiliated with Carnegie-Mellon University and the University of Pittsburgh. It is funded by a grant from the Richard King Mellon Foundation and supported by contributions from local industry. It also has received matching grants from Pennsylvania's Ben Franklin Partnership Program and retains a small percentage of companies that receive material support. The Enterprise Corporation provides hands-on assistance to tenant companies, creates links to business contacts, and develops educational programs for entrepreneurs. It has a board of directors and an advisory board. The corporation leverages support from universities, state governments, large corporations, financial institutions, investors, advisers, and government programs.

Control Data Business and Technology Centers (CDBTC) is a franchise operation of the Fortune 500 computer company, Control Data Corporation. With 22 operating incubators and more than seven years' experience, CDBTC seek to provide a full range of support services for seed or start-up phase business. The goal of these centers is to reduce the failure rate of new businesses. Since the first center opened in 1979, more than 90 percent of the businesses that have operated in the centers have survived and are growing, according to CDC. Control Data is unique in that it provides some services that other new business incubators cannot, such as sophisticated computers and access to Control Data PLATO computer-based education. The company currently has over 2 million square feet of space operating, with 738 companies and 6,100 employees.

Key Research Findings

A number of studies are beginning to shed light on the incubator concept. The first major survey of incubators—a fifty-incubator survey—was conducted by Candace Campbell and Mihailo Temali through the Hubert H. Humphrey Institute of Public Affairs at the University of Minnesota.[5] According to the survey, most incubators at that time were established in existing, and frequently vacant, buildings. Many had been purchased and reno-vated with the assistance of funding by a variety of government loans and grants. Others had been purchased with state or locally issued industrial rev-enue bonds. A few buildings had been donated or sold cheaply by private corporations.

Most of the incubators acted as brokers between new business and po-tential investors by making introductions to key people or by assisting in the development of proposals and loan packages. Publicly sponsored incubators sought primarily to create jobs, and university-affiliated incubators sought to transfer research and development activities and to spin off university re-search efforts.

The Temali-Campbell study identified a number of elements in incubator operations: flexibility in leasing and management of space, centralized ser-vices to help reduce overhead costs of tenant companies, and various types of business assistance. It is interesting that the research also discovered a unique social atmosphere that encouraged trading relationships.

In September 1985, David N. Allen, from the Institute of Public Admin-istration at the Pennsylvania State University, completed a special report for the Economic Development Administration Research and Evaluation Divi-sion of the U.S. Department of Commerce.[6] The study, "Small Business In-cubators and Enterprise Development," reported on a survey of 46 incubators and 217 tenant firms operating at the start of 1985.

Allen's concept of an incubator comprised four dimensions:

1. An organization or network of organizations providing people with busi-ness skills and knowledge and motivating them to start companies.

2. A tie to "U.S. real estate experience with building or renovating and man-aging multi-tenant facilities."

3. A way to "provide business consulting services to small business clients."

4. "Shared office services and rental space available for small businesses."

The study identified three organizational types of incubators: public and nonprofit, private, and university. It also identified three general categories of services provided to tenants: logistical or physical, shared office support, and management consulting. After analysis of the number and types of ten-ants, size of facilities, source of support, entry and exit routes, and types of services provided, the study concluded that "almost twice as many firms suc-ceed as fail." Success meant a firm moving out of the incubator; failure meant a firm discontinuing operations while in the incubator.

A third major project, "Innovation and Enterprise: A Study of NSF's In-novation Centers Program," was prepared for the National Science Founda-tion (NSF) and submitted to NSF in December 1985.[7] It reported on the programmatic activities and the viability of nine federally funded centers, the first of which was started in 1973.

The study found that the long-term financial survival of the eight existing centers is "still precarious, and financial viability is still a major center preoccupation." It reached five tentative conclusions:

1. "Support for an Innovation Center within a university budget is unlikely, unless the university has strong economic development ties with the local community."

2. The belief that a center can become self-sustaining by obtaining an equity position in tenant companies has not yet been confirmed. Ten years of external funding may be required before the equity mechanism works.

3. Five to ten years should be allowed before expecting strong economic development results from a center functioning with public funds.

4. Most public funding cycles are not congruent with center development, since the cycles range from two to five years between elections.

5. Some center activities may be supported on a fee-for-service basis, but strong management and networking skills are necessary.

According to the study, the effort to develop viable companies has, to this point, met with mixed results at best. In terms of program activities for tenant companies, however, it concluded that "there is good reason to argue that the Innovation Centers' business assistance efforts were successful, overall." Evidence suggested "real linkages between innovation and entrepreneurship education and later outcomes."

Overview of This Book

This book moves from a conceptual framework for incubators to specific data on their operation.

Chapter 2 provides a framework for viewing the development of the incubator concept. It relates the role of incubators to the emergence of entrepreneurs in the context of economic development. It presents a model for the planning, development, and implementation of the incubator concept.

Chapters 3 and 4 discuss critical success factors from two perspectives. Chapter 3 focuses on ten factors important to the success of incubators. Chapter 4 analyzes four factors critical to the success of tenant companies within the incubator.

Chapters 5 and 6 provide a quantitative analysis of the data from our national survey. Chapter 5 examines the structure and financing of incubators, and chapter 6 deals with selection and management issues.

Chapter 7 presents several case studies of operating incubators. It groups the studies according to four classifications: private, corporate/franchise, community, and university-related.

Chapter 8 provides an assessment of the future of new business incubators and their possible role in and contribution to entrepreneurial support and economic development.

The appendix presents a handbook approach to starting a new business incubator. Finally, a bibliography is included for reference purposes.

This book links theory with practice in providing an analysis of the incubator concept. It is hoped that the approach will enhance our knowledge and understanding of incubators, provide insights for both incubator operators and tenant company entrepreneurs, and present valuable data for scholars who might undertake future research.

Notes

1. "Business Incubators Proliferating in United States," *Economic Developer* 12(December 1985):12.

2. Edmund L. Andrews, "How Much for a Security Blanket?" *Venture* 8(February 1986):49–52.

3. A number of these overviews are adapted from descriptions in George Kozmetsky, Michael D. Gill, Jr., and Raymond W. Smilor, *Financing and Managing Fast-Growth Companies: The Venture Capital Process* (Lexington, Mass.: Lexington Books, 1985), 54–64.

4. Robert Frick, "Incubators Provide Cozy Starting Site," *USA Today,* March 12, 1986, pp. 1–2 of Money section.

5. Mihailo Temali and Candace Campbell, *Business Incubator Profiles: A National Survey* (Minneapolis: University of Minnesota, Hubert H. Humphrey Institute of Public Affairs, 1984). See, also, Candace Campbell, "Hatching Small Businesses," *Planning* 50(May 1984).

6. David N. Allen, "Small Business Incubators and Enterprise Development," Final Report, prepared for the Economic Development Administration Research and Evaluation Division, U.S. Department of Commerce, September 1985.

7. Mary Ann Scheirer, Veronica F. Nieva, Gregory H. Gaertner, Paul D. Newman, and Vivian F. Ramsey, "Innovation and Enterprise: A Study of NSF's Innovation Centers Program," Report prepared for the National Science Foundation, December 1985.

2
Incubators, Entrepreneurs, and Economic Development

The new business incubator is being developed as an innovative approach to economic development. It is one facet of a technology-venturing process that is an emerging American response to changing economic conditions. Technology venturing is an entrepreneurial process by which institutions—universities, government, and the private sector—take and share risk in integrating and commercializing scientific research, new technologies, and business opportunities. It often links public sector initiatives and private sector investments to spur economic growth and diversification.

Incubators can contribute to and benefit from a set of building blocks that make the technology-venturing process possible. These blocks include a healthy venture capital industry, a solid financial base, adequate public and private infrastructures, a sound educational system, and an extensive business network.

The basic concept behind the new business incubator—whether technology-oriented or nontechnical, urban or rural, nonprofit or profit-making, public or private, locally owned or part of a chain—is to leverage entrepreneurial talent. The primary driver of new business ventures is neither the availability of funds nor the rate of technological advance; it is the entrepreneur. New business incubators seek to maximize the potential of entrepreneurial talent within a community by providing entrepreneurs with services and support that complement their natural talents and enable them to expand their potential. The incubator can thus be a significant link between the entrepreneur, especially one who is technology-oriented, and the commercialization of the product or service offered (see figure 2–1).

Small businesses are the single largest job-creation segment of our economy. A 1981 study conducted at the Massachusetts Institute of Technology found that between 1969 and 1976, nearly two-thirds of all new jobs were created by firms employing fewer than twenty individuals.[1] Furthermore, statistics show that jobs created by firms employing fewer than 100 people—still well within the limits of what is considered small business—account for

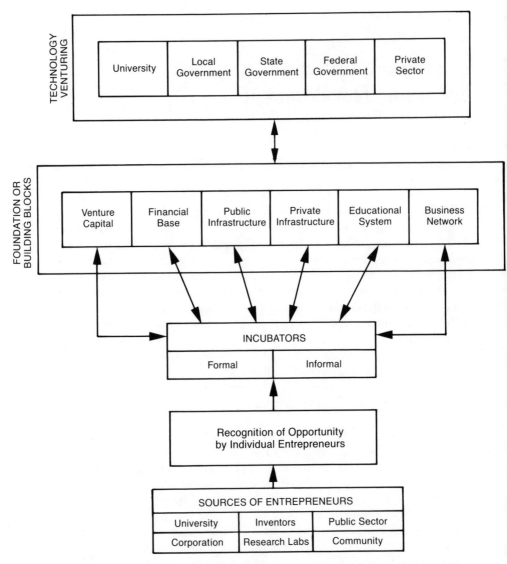

Figure 2–1. The Role of Incubators in Economic Development

nearly 80 percent of all new job creations. Since small business is good for economic development, the nurturing of small business should be an appropriate focus for economic policy. According to *The State of Small Business,* a 1984 Small Business Administration report to the president, "Small enterprises with under 20 employees generated all of the net new jobs in the economy between 1980 and 1982. Net employment grew by 984,000 jobs; enterprises of other sizes showed net employment declines during this period."[2] In addition, small firms and inventors are 2.4 times more productive per employee and twenty-four times more productive per dollar of research and development expenditure in the generation of innovation than are large firms.[3]

These developments must be weighed against another important fact—that nearly 50 percent of small businesses fail within five years. There are many reasons for businesses to fail: undercapitalization, poor management, technological obsolescence, fads, recession, competition, labor problems, inflation, and scarcity of raw materials. However, studies of small business that have focused on the reasons for business failure have found the key causes to be undercapitalization and poor management.[4] An estimated 2,000 businesses fold each year because of one serious error that was not foreseen. Nine out of ten small businesses fail because of management deficiencies—and research shows that nine out of ten causes of failure could have been foreseen.[5]

The new business incubator attempts to increase the chances of success for emerging companies.

The Entrepreneurial Process

Economic development is based on four critical factors:

1. Talent—people
2. Technology—ideas
3. Capital—resources
4. Know-how—knowledge

Entrepreneurial talent results from the drive, tenacity, dedication, and hard work of a special type of individual—people who make things happen. Entrepreneurs are people who recognize opportunities. Where there is a pool of talented entrepreneurial individuals, there is opportunity for growth, diversification, and new business development. There are a variety of sources for entrepreneurs: universities, corporations, research labs, communities, the public sector, and inventors of all sorts. Events that trigger the entrepreneurial push may include dissatisfaction with current employment, recognition

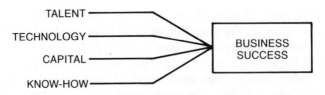

Figure 2–2. The Entrepreneurial Process

of an opportunity, an urge to try a new venture, changes in public policy, or simply a desire to promote an innovative idea.

But talent without ideas is like seed without water. The second critical component in the entrepreneurial process concerns the ability to generate ideas that have real potential within a reasonable time. The burst of creativity and innovation in emerging technological industries holds tremendous promise for economic development and technology business growth. When talent is linked with technology, people recognize and then push viable ideas, and the entrepreneurial process is underway.

Every dynamic process needs to be fueled. The fuel for the entrepreneurial process is capital. Capital is the catalyst in the entrepreneurial chain reaction. It is the lifeblood of emerging and expanding enterprises. In business, it is the sine qua non of a new product, an innovative service, or a brilliant idea. Capital provides the financial resources through which the ideas of the entrepreneur can be realized.

Along with talent, technology, and capital, one other element is indispensable to the successful entrepreneurial process. Know-how is the ability to leverage business or scientific knowledge in linking talent, technology, and capital in emerging and expanding enterprises. It is the ability to find and apply expertise in a variety of areas that can make the difference between success and failure. This expertise may involve management, marketing, finance, accounting, production, and manufacturing, as well as legal, scientific, and engineering help.

Successful entrepreneurial development requires a synergy among talent, technology, capital, and know-how (see figure 2–2). A new business incubator tries to be the integrating link that can increase the chances for success of new ventures for entrepreneurs. And incubators can provide a framework for focusing and binding the critical elements of the entrepreneurial process for new ventures. They can also significantly telescope the learning curve, thus giving entrepreneurs more time to let their businesses grow and more opportunities to learn from otherwise disastrous mistakes as they broaden their know-how.

Hypercompetition

Merely opening or establishing an incubator is not enough in today's environment. Businesses, even those that are being contemplated, must operate in a hypercompetitive environment. The business climate is fierce, both domestically and internationally. The competition is between countries, states, and communities, as well as between large and small firms and among industries. The environment in which emerging firms must operate is particularly unforgiving. The ability to introduce new technologies or services to the marketplace poses several unique competitive problems. There is a gap between the firm and its potential markets. This gap results from such issues as (1) public acceptance, (2) technological obsolescence, (3) social concerns, (4) channels of distribution, (5) development of an aftermarket, (6) overseas manufacturing, and (7) the process of moving to the next market.

To help companies meet the challenge of a hypercompetitive environment and to maximize the contributions of the small business and the technology business growth sectors to American society, the promotion of new business growth has become an important facet of economic policy at the federal, state, and local levels. Building indigenous companies has become an essential element in regional economic development.

Industrial relocation, long the central focus of regional economic development, tends to be a zero-sum game—one region or location benefits only at the expense of another. Indigenous company growth may be a more beneficial and necessary long-term economic development strategy for several reasons. First, it harnesses local entrepreneurial talent. Second, it builds companies, which, in turn, creates jobs and adds economic value to a region and community. Third, this strategy keeps home-grown talent—a scarce resource—within the community. Fourth, it encourages economic diversification and technological innovation by creating a climate that rewards productivity and innovation. In this context, new business technology incubators can be an important component in the development of an indigenous company strategy in a region or community (see figure 2–3).

Stimulants

A variety of social and economic factors are stimulating entrepreneurial activity and thus generating more robust economic development. These factors include an increasing focus on capital formation, changing institutional relationships, supportive government programs, reassessment of intellectual property, and new approaches to innovation (see figure 2–4).

A growing pool of capital dedicated to the entrepreneurial process is being created in the United States today. Much of the attention to this pool

Figure 2–3. Hypercompetition

has been focused on venture capital—a dynamic and creative process by which capital investments in mid-growth enterprises are made, managed, and developed. Venture capital is generally available only to firms with a proven track record. Venture capitalists rarely provide seed capital—that is, capital used to prove a concept, to build a prototype, or to permit an entrepreneur to start a new firm. Consequently, there need to be mechanisms to allow entrepreneurs to reach a point at which they might be able to tap the resources of the venture capital industry. New business incubators can provide one type of mechanism. They can serve an emerging company in two finan-

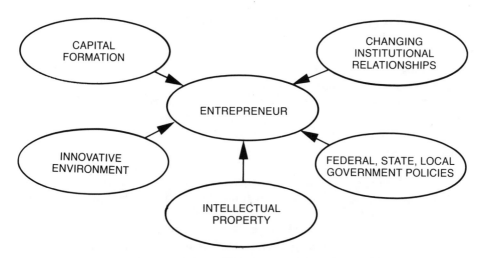

Figure 2–4. Stimulants for Entrepreneurial Activity

cially critical ways: they can provide financial resources to assist in the start-up phase of a company, and they can act as a facilitator for future financing as the company matures.

A second stimulator involves the commercialization of technology among various social institutions. The ability to transform scientific and technical developments into profitable business opportunities is at the heart of the commercialization process. Social institutions—government, industry, and nonprofit organizations—are important sources of research and development. Other institutions—government laboratories, industry, universities and colleges, and other nonprofit institutions—directly perform research and development functions. These institutions are looking for innovative ways to collaborate, to promote entrepreneurial activity, and to diffuse technology while they reap the rewards of their intellectual property assets. Within each of these institutions are potential entrepreneurs, for whom a technology incubator can provide the opportunity to commercialize their ideas and visions.

A third stimulant to the entrepreneurial process is the proactive role of federal, state, and local governments. The federal government is actively seeking to fund and support technological efforts that have the potential for commercialization. Through agency quotas or "set-asides" to small high technology companies, through innovative efforts at the Small Business Administration, through a growing emphasis on technology transfer at federal laboratories, and through innovative programs such as the Small Business Innovation Research Program, the federal government is encouraging high-technology small business formation and growth. State and local governments are also finding innovative mechanisms to support entrepreneurial activities: direct funding of research and development, development of high-technology initiatives, establishment of research and development parks and science centers, emphasis on quality educational programs, tax incentives, and an increasing emphasis on indigenous company formation and growth. Local governments are cooperating with state and federal government initiatives, even to the point of providing facilities, resources, and expertise to promote new business activity.

Fourth, universities, federal laboratories, industry, and research consortia are undertaking major reassessment of policies and approaches to intellectual property because of hypercompetition. This is particularly important to many emerging high-technology companies. Since each of these institutions is producing entrepreneurs who take their ideas and innovations to the marketplace, it is becoming more important to reassess patents, licenses, royalties, and the general ownership of scientific and technological developments. Given the growing collaborative relationships that are developing between business, government, and academia, and given their more direct attempts to transfer technology to the marketplace, there are likely to be increasing numbers of entrepreneurs seeking opportunities to commercialize their ideas and innovations.

A fifth stimulant to new business development is the removal of barriers to innovation through the establishment of an environment favorable to entrepreneurial activity. The removal of barriers has been accomplished on many levels, including federal, state, and local governments and industry. On the national level, the federal government has encouraged the transfer of technology from federal laboratories and has encouraged formation of research consortia by modifying antitrust laws. Many state governments have repealed tax laws that are considered disadvantageous to technology-oriented firms, have enacted special education laws to help keep and attract highly qualified personnel to local employment, and have endeavored to create an environment conducive to entrepreneurship. Many corporations, recognizing that entrepreneurship increases productivity, have established flexible corporate cultures to accommodate *intra*preneurial activity. Some have even established venture capital pools and incubator units to invest in entrepreially oriented employees.

The New Business Incubator

Successful entrepreneurship takes a wide variety of talents. However, it is rare to find a potential entrepreneur who combines the technical expertise necessary for technological innovation with the business acumen necessary for suc-

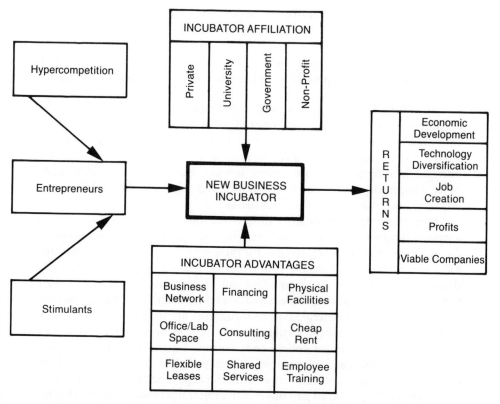

Figure 2–5. Inputs and Outputs of the New Business Incubator

cessful product commercialization. One concept that has developed in the last five years to facilitate the development of entrepreneurial creativity and education is the incubator unit (see figure 2–5).

Incubator units are designed to assist entrepreneurs in developing their business skills in an environment that promotes company development. Although incubators vary in the scope of assistance provided, there are some generic components to the incubator concept. After screening potential entrepreneurs, an incubator may provide low-cost office and laboratory space, administrative services, access to library and computer facilities, skilled consultants, an inexpensive work force in the form of graduate and undergraduate students, and special contacts with bankers, venture capitalists, technologists, and government officials. In this environment, aspiring entrepreneurs have more freedom to be creative, since their energies can be devoted to product development rather than to the rigors of obtaining financing or managing an organization. During this period, the entrepreneur is associated with other entrepreneurs who are facing similar difficulties, providing an association that should help solve problems and stimulate the entrepreneur's drive for success.

An incubator is not only an organization; it is also a physical unit. Incubators start as a single building or group of buildings in which participating entrepreneurs can be housed together to interact spontaneously. For a nominal fee, the institution sponsoring the incubator may provide secretarial support, duplicating services, accounting services, technical editing help, computer equipment, conference space, health and other benefit packages, and access to university facilities and expertise.

Organizationally, incubators differ from one another because of their varying priorities. Priorities are different because of the funding that supports the incubator unit. Funding sources for these units include federal, state, and local governments, communities, universities, private individuals and foundations, and corporations. Incubators can be associated with any of these funding sources to varying degrees and, therefore, have similar goals but different priorities. The general goals of incubators are to develop firms and to stimulate entrepreneurship. Incubators may seek to develop jobs, create investment opportunities for college endowments, expand a tax base for local government, enhance the image of college technical programs, speed the transfer of technological innovation from the academic and research worlds to industry, fill a perceived gap in venture capital financing by improving the quality of locally based entrepreneurial talent, and build a core of indigenous companies (see table 2–1).

Many of the first incubators are university related. The advantages of being on or near a university campus are numerous: library facilities; exposure to state-of-the-art technical thinking and equipment; access to undergraduates—a cheap and technically skilled labor pool; a creative environment; and potential employment as a lecturer. Companies within the incubator profit from the resources of the university in a variety of ways. They may benefit from having the best available talent when they need it without having to carry that high-priced talent on their payroll. And these companies receive the stimulus and catalytic effect associated with working alongside exceptional professionals from outside their organization.

Science parks may accompany the incubator unit as another link between universities and industry. Located near universities, these parks have as their objective the attraction of both research and development and the manufacturing facilities of established technology-based companies. Science parks, also called technology or research parks, act as lightning rods for technology-based companies and can be an area's lure for attracting companies and in-

Table 2–1
Incubator Goals and Orientations

Type of Incubator	Jobs	Profit	Economic Development	Economic Diversification	Tax Base Expansion	Image	Investment Opportunity
				Priorities			
University-related		X		X		X	X
Community-sponsored	X		X	X	X		
Federal technology transfer	X					X	
Corporate-affiliated		X					X
Privately sponsored		X					X
Public/Private	X	X	X	X			X

dividuals from out of state. Science parks may also give a university a method of further benefiting from the development of firms incubated in its facilities, since these firms are prime candidates for research park tenants.

To understand how the incubator concept works in practice, it is necessary to consider a range of factors critical to their success and to the success of tenant companies within the incubator.

Notes

1. Mihailo Temali and Candace Campbell, *Business Incubator Profiles: A National Survey* (Minneapolis: University of Minnesota, Hubert H. Humphrey Institute of Public Affairs, 1984), 2.

2. U.S. Small Business Administration, *The State of Small Business* (Washington, D.C.: 1984), United States Government Printing Office, 25.

3. *Starting a Small Business Incubator: A Handbook for Sponsors and Developers.* (Washington, D.C.: U.S. Small Business Administration, Region V, and the Office of Private Sector Initiatives, 1984), 1.

4. IC² Institute, Surveys on Small Business, 1981–83.

5. *Starting a Small Business Incubator.*

3
Critical Success Factors: The Incubator Perspective

N ew business incubators are diverse in their purposes, organizational structures, operating policies, and institutional affiliations. Nevertheless, a number of critical success factors are common to the development and operation of all incubators. In our national survey, on-site reviews, and extensive discussions with those involved in incubation development, a number of key ideas and practices emerged as important in the incubation experience. As shown in figure 3–1, these key ideas and practices have been organized into ten critical success factors:

On-site business expertise

Access to financing and capitalization

In-kind financial support

Community support

Entrepreneurial network

Entrepreneurial education

Perception of success

Selection process for tenants

Tie to a university

Concise program milestones with clear policies and procedures

Not all successful incubators incorporate all of these factors, but there does seem to be direct correlation between successful incubator development and the extent to which each of these factors is consciously implemented by most incubator managements. The more extensively these factors are incorporated into the incubator, the greater the chance of success for the tenant companies and the incubator of which they are a part.

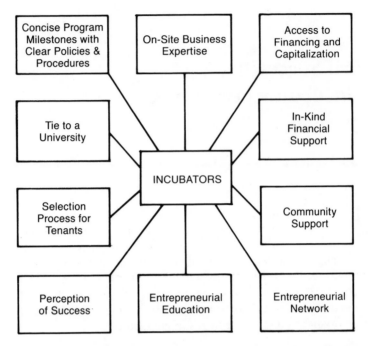

Figure 3–1. Ten Success Factors for Incubator Development

On-Site Business Expertise

Emerging companies require business expertise. Very often they will have the talent, ideas, and even the capital to launch a new venture, but they most often lack, in various degrees, the business know-how to transform these assets into viable business enterprises.

The importance of this expertise was reinforced in our national survey. The consulting services considered most important to tenant companies included, in order of importance, business planning, marketing, accounting, and management. When *important* and *most important* evaluations are combined, management and marketing support rank highest (see chapter 6).

The marketing function is essential in differentiating the products of the company and in establishing the credibility of the firm in a highly competitive environment. Marketing is especially difficult in technologically innovative companies, particularly when they are addressing new needs and markets. Marketing must deal with several problems unique to technologically based companies:

Technological obsolescence.

Hesitation to buy early-generation technologies.

The uncertainty of selecting the right initial market for a new technology where there is the potential for multiple applications across a variety of industries.

The need to educate potential users.

Difficulties in forecasting market demand for innovative products for which users may have little or no frame of reference.

Management determines how emerging companies will respond to changes in the marketplace and, especially, how effectively they will deal with growth. Managing human, financial, and technological resources demands skills that entrepreneurs very often have to learn and then hone through experience.

Business planning in the incubator requires that emerging companies look past their first product. They need to anticipate new products and chart the general direction and future needs of the company. Planning may include not only the growth of the firm but also its eventual acquisition by a larger company.

The accounting function is a key part of control and oversight in start-up ventures. It is particularly important to tenant companies in coming to grips with cash flow. No matter how wonderful income projections may appear, it is cash flow that determines whether and how long a company survives. It is more important than the ultimate bottom line; it is the survival barometer. New enterprises must become acutely aware of cash-flow analysis.

Regardless of the form incubators take, they should provide on-site business expertise, and they can do this in a variety of ways. The know-how that is internally available in incubators may be leveraged into tenant companies through:

An incubator director or president who brings experience and professional management and marketing savvy to the incubator.

A board of directors that encompasses a range and mix of expertise that can be passed on to tenant companies.

An advisory council made up of key professionals to whom the tenant companies have access.

A consultant network that can provide services, often on a favorable fee basis.

Access to Financing and Capitalization

Capital is the lifeblood of emerging companies. Consequently, access to working-capital financing and equity and debt capitalization comprise the second tier of consulting services considered most important to tenant companies. In order of priority, the necessary access includes evaluation of financial options, access to loans and grants, loan packaging, and introduction to venture capital institutions and venture capitalists (see chapter 6).

With the range and complexity of financing alternatives in today's marketplace, companies need assistance in understanding the alternatives and in determining which may be best for them. The ability to distinguish and appreciate how start-up entrepreneurs can benefit or lose through any particular financial option is important in launching and developing a new venture. Commercial banking, investment banking, Small Business Administration support, research and development limited partnerships, and private investors, to name a few alternatives, all present different advantages and disadvantages that need to be identified and evaluated. This process involves not only an understanding of the technical and financial dimensions of an alternative but also the ability to recognize the attitudes, perspectives, and concerns—the mind-set—of those providing funds. This is particularly true when a company considers trading equity for control.

Many emerging companies finance their early development through personal loans and government grants. Consequently, a number of incubators try to provide access to individuals, institutions, and agencies that provide loans and grants. *Access* here implies the ability to get to the right person and to move more expeditiously. Sources of loans and grants include traditional funding mechanisms, such as banks, and newer mechanisms, such as the federal Small Business Innovation Research Program and key individuals, or "angels," in the community.

Most entrepreneurs who start companies are not very experienced in dealing with banks and other lending institutions. The ability to package a loan or an application for a grant, therefore, is an important service that can be provided to tenant companies.

Finally, most incubator leaders think it is important to provide tenant companies with introductions to the venture capital industry. This is especially important after a company has developed in the incubator for a time. Very few venture capital firms are interested in start-up companies, and most do not make seed-capital investments. Because start-up companies require a great deal of help, have a higher chance of failure, take up a great deal of staff time, and have little management or marketing experience, most venture capital firms prefer to make investments in more developed enterprises.

Some venture capital firms do set aside a small amount of their venture pool, perhaps 3 percent to 10 percent, to make selected seed-capital investments, and some funds devoted to seed capital are being developed. But most venture capitalists prefer to wait until a company has a track record, proven management, and demonstrated market competence before investing. Consequently, an incubator can provide an important link to the venture capital community by focusing early attention on tenant companies, by making introductions as the company proves itself in the marketplace, and, especially, by educating the entrepreneur to the venture capital process and the mind-set of the venture capitalist.

Incubators can be a source of and can provide access to seed capital, the most difficult type of funding to generate. Our national survey showed that a variety of community-related sources provide financial assistance to incubators, which, in turn, pass on some of those resources to tenant companies. In addition, some state and federal government financial support is being directed to new business incubators.

In-Kind Financial Support

One type of seed-capital financing that incubators provide to tenant companies is financial assistance through in-kind service support. These in-kind services include secretarial, administrative, and facilities support. The most important secretarial services to tenant companies, in order of importance, are photocopying, receptionist duties, word processing, and general typing. The key administrative services are equipment rental, mailing, accounting help, and contract administration. The most important shared-facilities services are the miscellaneous type, such as janitorial and parking; next come security, computers, loading dock, and conference room services. See chapter 6 for more on this subject.

By assisting with secretarial, administrative, and facilities services, incubators help provide a range of basic but much needed services that start-up companies require but cannot afford or often neglect or ignore.

Tenant companies pay the cost of these services in a variety of ways. The incubator may provide a relatively low or subsidized rent to the tenant companies. It may charge a competitive rent but tie access to services into the rental agreement. It may provide these services for an equity share in the company, or the tenant company may be charged only on an as-used basis, which helps keep its costs down. As part of the arrangement, most incubators provide extremely flexible lease terms. Chapter 5 has more on these arrangements.

Community Support

Community support plays an important role in sustaining incubator development. Most incubators in some way reflect a community's effort to diversify its economy, create jobs, and leverage entrepreneurial talent for a more viable long-term economy. Part of the process, however, involves recognizing that companies take time to develop. Economies do not change overnight—and an incubator should be only one tool in a broader economic development plan.

Our national survey showed that there is indeed some evidence that incubators contribute to the process of building indigenous companies. That is, they can keep home-grown talent at home to develop companies that help generate jobs for the community. Since the incubator concept is relatively new, not many companies have actually graduated or left the incubators. However, of the thirty companies in the national survey that had graduated from incubators 20 percent remained in the same neighborhood as the incubator, 60 percent in the same city, and 20 percent in the same state* (see chapter 6). No doubt, some companies will be lured to other states or will opt to move in the future. But early indications are that incubators may be a viable economic development tool.

Because of this, incubators do gain the financial, moral, and public relations support of communities. This support may come from private individuals, city government, private industrial councils, county government, universities, and chambers of commerce. This support is also crucial in gaining additional assistance from professionals and others in the community who may be able to provide business expertise to the tenant companies. When the incubator is perceived as a reflection of community goals and as a potential asset to economic development and diversification, it is able, to a degree, to rise above self-interest and thus garner more broad-based support.

The Entrepreneurial Network

Entrepreneurship is a dynamic process. As such, it requires links, or relationships, not only with individuals but also with a variety of institutions. The stronger, more complex, and more diverse the web of relationships, the more the entrepreneur is likely to have access to opportunities, the greater the chance of solving problems expeditiously, and, ultimately, the greater the chance of success for a new venture.

The entrepreneurial network depicted in figure 3–2 illustrates some of

---

*Control Data Business and Technology Centers has indicated that they have graduated 353 companies, but no data on these companies was available.

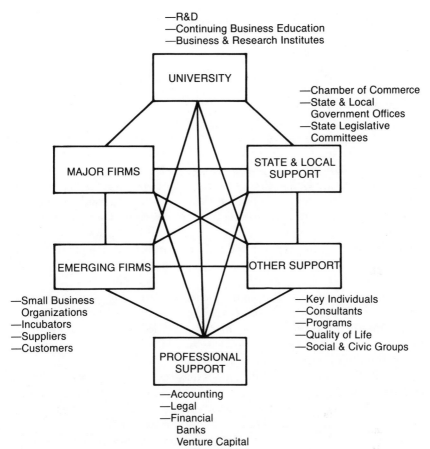

—R&D
—Continuing Business Education
—Business & Research Institutes

UNIVERSITY

—Chamber of Commerce
—State & Local
   Government Offices
—State Legislative
   Committees

MAJOR FIRMS

STATE & LOCAL SUPPORT

EMERGING FIRMS

OTHER SUPPORT

—Small Business
   Organizations
—Incubators
—Suppliers
—Customers

—Key Individuals
—Consultants
—Programs
—Quality of Life
—Social & Civic Groups

PROFESSIONAL SUPPORT

—Accounting
—Legal
—Financial
   Banks
   Venture Capital

Figure 3–2. The Entrepreneurial Network

the potential links and relationships that can promote and sustain new ventures in an incubator. A university provides business and research centers, continuing business education (especially in management and marketing skills), and a potential base for research and development that also helps develop entrepreneurs. Major firms provide key credibility to emerging companies as customers and are sources of spin-off opportunities. Emerging firms are provided with a tier of peer support, find critical help in peer organizations, and establish important links with suppliers and customers. Through networks, professional support comes from accountants, lawyers, and financiers. State and local government provide incentives, direct aid, and access to contracts, while responding to the creative pressures of emerging business interest groups. Other support networks take a variety of forms: key individuals, consultants, workshops and business education programs, social and civic groups, and collective efforts to improve quality-of-life factors.

Incubators can advance tenant company development by providing the interface for a broader and richer range of networking opportunities to entrepreneurs.

Entrepreneurial Education

If tenant companies are to succeed in a hypercompetitive environment, they must eventually stand on their own. At some point, they must leave the security of the incubator—and this is not easy to do.

One persistent problem that most incubators encounter is the reluctance of tenant companies to move out on their own. It is difficult to leave the protected environment of the incubator. The expectations of tenant companies for continued support, the reinforcement of peers, the ability to tap business expertise, and the general comfort of working in a familiar environment—all this can make the process of graduation from the incubator a difficult one.

To deal with this problem, many incubators are addressing the need for entrepreneurial education. Entrepreneurial education helps prepare the entrepreneur to do business outside the incubator by developing the skills (instilling some of the necessary know-how) so that entrepreneurs can extend their own abilities in running a company.

Training and education in incubators may be through a formal and structured program of both theoretical and how-to topics, or it may be through an informal process of interaction, discussion, and exchange. Programs may be developed in-house, related to continuing education efforts in a university, or provided by consultants, academics, and experienced practitioners. Training and education activities may address a variety of topics: estate planning, tax advice, business planning, product development, marketing techniques, management skills, competitive contract bidding, grant application, and accounting practices.

Part of the education process also occurs through peer interaction. The opportunity to meet and talk with other entrepreneurs who have experienced and solved similar problems or have faced similar business situations is a valuable learning experience that incubators can help provide.

The Perception of Success

An important, intangible element in incubator development is the need to create a perception of success. This perception can help establish the incubator as a resource for the community. It can also help position the tenant companies in the market. If the incubator is perceived as successful, it can attract resources more easily, get stronger start-up ventures interested, and help tenant companies build credibility.

There are a variety of ways to establish a perception of success:

A new and attractive facility

Affiliation with key institutions, both public and private, in the area

An experienced (successful) incubator manager

A board of key directors

A noted advisory council

A group of promising start-up companies

Successful graduated firms

By inference (who is associated with the incubator), by reference (what others say about the incubator and its tenants), and, ultimately, by evidence (what the incubator actually produces), a perception of success can be established that serves both the incubator and the tenant companies.

The Selection Process for Tenants

If an incubator seeks to build companies, it must have a selection process through which it evaluates, recommends, and selects tenant firms. By what criteria will it admit companies into the incubator? How will the incubator judge success? When and under what circumstances will it "pull the plug" on tenant companies? What, if any, exit policy exists, and how does this apply to the selection of incoming firms?

The criteria for tenant selection are important and may vary with the mission and objectives of the incubator. Criteria may include:

The potential to grow

The ability to create jobs

A focus on a specific industry

An ability to pay operating expenses

A business plan

Market analysis

A cash flow statement

Unless there is some set of criteria by which to evaluate tenant company development, there is no frame of reference for determining whether a company is on or off track and no way to decide whether and to what degree it may need additional resources.

Most incubators have established some process by which firms are reviewed and approved for admission into the facility. Usually, the incubator manager or a selection committee is involved in the review process. In some cases, the board of directors becomes involved. Admission to the incubator often requires a decision by the board or by the incubator manager. In some cases (see chapter 5), a selection committee may be involved.

There are exceptions to all selection criteria. But it is important to note that the clearer and the more developed the set of selection criteria, the greater the likelihood of admitting companies that can be successful.

Tie to a University

Most incubators have established ties to a university. In our national survey, over 80 percent of the incubators had some kind of affiliation with a university. These ties have developed because the relationship has proved to be mutually beneficial.

The ties can be formal or informal. The incubator may actually be a part of the university or a particular college. In this case, the facility may be on campus, and the incubator may be subject to the rules and regulations of the university system. Through an informal affiliation, the incubator may be on campus but operate as an independent entity that leases space from the university. In addition, incubators have developed other types of university ties that include having former university professors as managers or advisers or having university faculty entrepreneurs in the tenant companies.

Although incubators benefit from the direct and indirect support of a university, there are also advantages to a university from a relationship with an incubator. The incubator provides a mechanism for commercializing university research. It helps a university partly fulfill an emerging obligation to contribute directly to economic development. It also provides an opportunity for university faculty and graduate students to do research on business development, especially through longitudinal studies.

Because of the potential mutually beneficial nature of the incubator–university relationship, most incubators in our national survey are physically close to a university. That is, they are five to ten minutes by car, within walking distance, or on campus.

Concise Program Milestones with Clear Policies and Procedures

Whether and how rapidly companies develop in an incubator is partly dependent on the "chemistry" between those managing the incubator and the entrepreneurs in the tenant companies. Tenant companies need to know what will be expected of them, what the incubator will provide, how they will be evaluated, and what the day-to-day procedures and general operating policies of the incubator will be. These issues become all the more important for tenant companies in those incubators that take an equity position in the incoming firms.

All emerging companies experience problems and uncertainties. To help minimize the difficulties, it is important for incubator management to communicate and for entrepreneurs to understand the program milestones by which tenant company performance will be measured, as well as the incubator's policies and procedures for dealing with tenant company development.

The relationship between the incubator and the tenant company can be a sensitive one, especially if the expectations of each party are different or if there is confusion over what each contributes to and what each gets from the association. Consequently, the more concise the program milestones and the clearer the policies and procedures, the greater the likelihood that expectations on both sides will be met, that misunderstandings will be minimized, and that each side will benefit from the relationship.

4
Critical Success Factors:
The Tenant Company Perspective

M aking the entrepreneurial leap—the wholehearted, all-out, no-holds-barred commitment to a new enterprise—requires guts, dedication, and savvy. It takes a willingness to experiment, a capacity to learn, and an inclination to take risks. That is why entrepreneurs are a special breed. But what drives these unconventional men and women?[1] Why do they march to the beat of a different drummer? If incubator developers and managers are to help build companies, they need to know about the makings of an entrepreneur and the dynamics of entrepreneurship.[2]

The entrepreneur has an uncanny ability to perceive emerging needs in the market. To meet those needs, he innovates. He develops new products or services, finds new methods of production, identifies new markets, discovers new sources of supply, and creates new forms of organization. The entrepreneur can even take an old idea and transform it into an exciting business venture. He has a sixth sense, springing from the application of insight and initiative, for what will succeed in a hypercompetitive environment. By continually taking the pulse of the marketplace, he can capitalize on business opportunities that might otherwise be missed.

The entrepreneur is a doer. He implements. His determination to succeed is reflected in a constant sense of urgency, in a basic need to be in control of his own destiny, and in an inherent attraction to challenges.[3] Obstacles are simply problems to be overcome; failures are merely temporary setbacks. Consequently, the entrepreneur is the real driver behind new business development, economic growth, and job creation.

Going into business for oneself is a life-affecting decision. The entrepreneur cuts the umbilical cord of job security to opt for personal independence, to be his own boss. Consequently, the business becomes the most important thing in the entrepreneur's life. It is the focus of all his energy. He lives and breathes the company, thinks about it at home and at night, and is willing to work sixty or seventy or eighty hours a week for small wages for long pe-

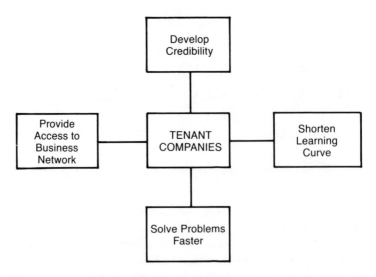

Figure 4–1. The Benefit of Incubators to Tenant Companies

riods. Time is subserviant to success, so entrepreneurship can be tough on marriages and on private lives.

Entrepreneurs want to do their own thing. As a result, they thrive on activity and take satisfaction in the success of their companies. Their achievement orientation and problem-solving abilities go a long way toward overcoming barriers to success.

Entrepreneurs take calculated risks. They are not gamblers, however, and rarely bet the company on one roll of the dice. They generally assess problems before they act and are well aware of alternatives and contingencies.

By understanding the entrepreneur and by knowing the dynamics of the entrepreneurial process, incubators can more effectively utilize resources to help develop companies. Incubators should provide, and entrepreneurs should expect to receive, important benefits that cannot be provided as expeditiously, affectively, or in such a timely manner outside the incubator. As shown in figure 4–1, incubators can and should provide four key benefits to tenant companies. They can and should

Develop credibility

Shorten the learning curve

Solve problems faster

Provide access to the business network

Develop Credibility

A start-up firm faces a particularly difficult problem in a hypercompetitive environment: it must establish its credibility as a viable company. A new venture must somehow demonstrate that it has staying power; that it will be here next year; that it can service its contracts; and that it can fulfill obligations in the long term, not just the short term. It must therefore gain recognition in the marketplace. Without recognition, there is no credibility. And without credibility, a new firm cannot establish effective relationships upon which to develop and grow.

Every potential customer, client, or user of a company's product or service has a degree of fear, uncertainty, and doubt. The problem is intensified in dealing with a firm that one has never heard of before. Will this new firm be in existence next year? Can it deliver on time? Can it provide service when needed? Is it reliable? Are the products and services of high quality? Will doing business with this new company jeopardize the buyer's job? The lower the credibility of the company, the higher the degree of fear, uncertainty, and doubt in the customer.

Incubators can help build credibility in new businesses. If the incubator has a positive reputation, community support, and, especially, a demonstrated record of producing viable companies, then a start-up venture's association with the incubator establishes a strategic relationship for the new enterprise. A strategic relationship is a mutually beneficial tie between the two entities in which each maintains its unique character and culture while enhancing the goals and objectives of both. A kind of business symbiosis occurs. Each entity is both dependent on and independent of the other. The strategic relationship may, for example, open a new market for one firm and provide access to a new technology for the other. It is interesting that the relationship can enhance the credibility of both because it provides resources, strengths, or capabilities that neither may have on its own.

In the incubator–tenant strategic relationship, the incubator admits a company that it believes will help fulfill its own goals and objectives. At the same time, the tenant company acquires the credibility of being chosen to be part of the incubator. With that selection, the tenant company can differentiate itself from those outside the incubator, can show that it has access to a variety of resources that will help sustain it, can link itself with community objectives, and can thus tap sources of support that may give it an edge in the marketplace. In other words, the tenant company can demonstrate credibility that it might not have or that might be far more difficult to acquire if it were not part of the incubator.

In addition to the strategic relationship, an incubator can help provide credibility to start-up companies in other ways. Word-of-mouth is like wildfire in industry, particularly in high-technology industries. Positive word-of-mouth can create excitement and build expectations; negative word-of-mouth can devastate a product or kill a company. Through their own networks and contacts, the incubator manager, board of directors, advisers, and consultants have the opportunity to spread the word on a new company. They may talk about an innovative product, a quality service, the experience of the management team, or the unique capabilities of the entrepreneur. By doing so, they help build credibility for the new venture.

Through this process, those associated with the incubator management may even provide access to a key customer, whose dealings with the start-up firm then provide credibility by association. There is a perception that the start-up company must be a viable business if this key customer has decided to buy its product or use its service. By helping to develop the credibility of the tenant company, the incubator can help overcome a major difficulty for start-up ventures.

Shorten the Learning Curve

If tenant companies are to grow and eventually stand on their own in the tough real world, entrepreneurs need to learn how to run a company. The learning process must extend the enthusiasm, dedication, and start-up talents of the entrepreneur and must encompass that know-how and those business skills that are more and more necessary as a company develops—management, marketing, accounting, business planning. But the learning process can sometimes take a long time, and time is precious.

Incubators can help accelerate the learning process. They can condense experience. Through entrepreneurial education, the management of tenant companies can tap the know-how of more knowledgeable and experienced business people. In the process, they can shorten their own learning curve.

Programs dealing with the various aspects of management can address issues related to planning, organizing, controlling, and monitoring business development. Those dealing with marketing can examine topics such as positioning, segmentation, pricing, distribution, and promotion and advertising. Other programs can deal with issues related to finance and accounting. These programs may be formal seminars, scheduled presentations, ad hoc meetings with those "in the know," discussion sessions, one-on-one meetings with incubator management, or peer interactions.

The purpose of this entrepreneurial education is to compress experience, to shorten the entrepreneur's learning curve, and to reinforce continually the notion that the entrepreneur is ultimately responsible for the company and must eventually run it on his own.

Solve Problems Faster

In a hypercompetitive environment, start-up companies do not have the luxury of time. They cannot afford to reinvent the wheel. If problems are not solved expeditiously, the start-up venture is in trouble.

Time is compressed even further for technologically innovative companies. Product life cycles are no longer twenty, or thirty, or forty years. A new technology may have a life cycle of perhaps eighteen months before it becomes obsolete, or a major firm grabs it up, or the need in the market changes. Consequently, new companies benefit from the ability to solve problems fast—whether the problem is a technological hitch, an engineering difficulty, a financial constraint, or a marketing limitation.

Incubators have the ability to solve problems faster for tenant companies. By targeting the right problem, locating the appropriate individual or group to assist, and then helping to implement the solution, incubator management can play an important role in assisting tenant company development. If the incubator can facilitate the acquisition of a loan, assist in correctly filling out applications for government grants, locate a person with specific management skills, speed the development of a prototype product—in other words, if it can help solve problems faster—the tenant company has a higher likelihood of success.

Provide Access to the Business Network

Successful entrepreneurs are good network builders. Indeed, the entrepreneurial process is embedded in networks of social relationships. Within these networks, entrepreneurship is facilitated or constrained by linkages among entrepreneurs, resources, and opportunities. For entrepreneurs, the critical link is to opportunities; for managers, it is to resources.

The incubator, by providing access to a much broader business network, may serve both purposes. It may strengthen the link to opportunities for the entrepreneur, and it may increase the resources available to entrepreneurs as they become managers. Essentially, the incubator can extend the networking capabilities of entrepreneurs. Through the incubator manager, the board of directors, advisers, consultants, and peers, the entrepreneurs in tenant companies can have more direct and indirect access to the business network of a community, region, and industry.

The more effectively incubators can provide access to the business network and the more conscientiously entrepreneurs seek to develop it, the more tenant companies are likely to find opportunities and take advantage of resources.

The benefits that incubators provide to tenant companies can vary considerably. The prices for the benefits can also be dramatically different. Consequently, entrepreneurs need to carefully evaluate the range and degree of the available benefits. If the incubator does, indeed, develop the credibility of the new company, shorten the learning curve of the entrepreneur, solve the emerging company's problems expeditiously, and provide effective access to a business network, the company will acquire benefits inside the incubator that it might not have outside.

Notes

1. Women comprise the fastest growing segment of entrepreneurs in the United States today. In fact, they are increasing at six times the rate of men. The generic "he" is used here to refer to both men and women entrepreneurs. For a discussion of women as entrepreneurs, see Robert D. Hisrich and Candida G. Brush, *The Woman Entrepreneur* (Lexington, Mass.: Lexington Books, 1985).

2. To review the latest research on entrepreneurship, see Donald L. Sexton and Raymond W. Smilor, eds., *The Art and Science of Entrepreneurship* (Cambridge, Mass.: Ballinger, 1986).

3. For a discussion of these and other characteristics of entrepreneurs, see John A. Welsh, "Entrepreneurial Characteristics: The Driving Force," in Raymond W. Smilor and Robert L. Kuhn, eds., *Corporate Creativity* (New York: Praeger, 1984).

5
Structure and Financing

Chapters 5 and 6 present the results of our national survey on incubators. The data provide insights into the structure, operation, and diversity of this innovative approach to business development.

Data on new business incubators in America were collected by means of a mail survey. The survey was conducted in July and August 1985. Traditional mail-survey research techniques and procedures were employed in collecting the data, including follow-up telephone calls and questionnaires to nonrespondents.

The original sample consisted of 117 incubators that had been identified from a variety of sources, including a data base developed at the IC^2 Institute, the U.S. Small Business Administration, published reports, and individuals. This sample included all the operating or planned incubators in the United States at that time. Responses were received from fifty incubators. This represents an effective response rate of 43 percent.

Participation and Review

A wide variety of institutional types have been active in initiating new business incubators. As shown in figure 5–1, 54.5 percent of the owners or sponsors of new business incubators are from the private for-profit sector, 22 percent from local government, 9.8 percent from universities, 6.5 percent from state governments, 5.7 percent from private nonprofit entities, and 1.6 from the federal government.

Incubator managers, boards of directors, and special selection committees play key roles in recommending, reviewing, and approving companies for inclusion in the incubator. In most incubators (86.5 percent), incubator managers are actively involved in recommending tenant companies. For 33.3 percent of the respondents, selection committees are active; for 30.4 percent, the board of directors is active. For 50 percent of the incubators, other groups or individuals recommend companies (figure 5–2).

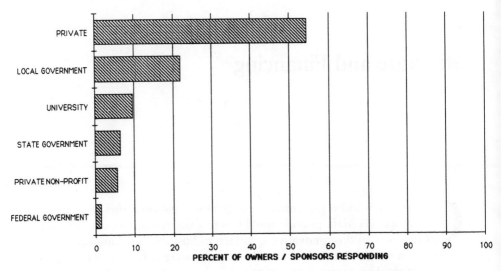

Figure 5–1. Incubator Owner's or Sponsor's Affiliation

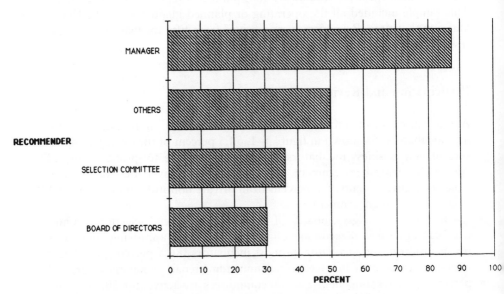

I **Figure 5–4. Owner's Involvement in Incubator**

After recommendation, potential tenant companies are reviewed. In over 80 percent of the incubators, the manager is involved in the review process, and in 53 percent, the selection committee is involved. In over 30 percent of the cases, the board of directors is involved.

Final approval is given by the board of directors in 64 percent of the incubators that responded, by the managers in 59.3 percent, and by the selection committee in 44 percent. In 42.9 percent of the incubators, others are involved in the final approval process (figure 5–3).

Owners are involved in incubators in a variety of ways. They take both active and passive roles in the incubator and in the tenant companies. As shown in figure 5–4, the primary responsibilities of owners are as follows: 88 percent of the owners from the responding incubators provide financial support; 77 percent serve as board members for the incubator; and 75 percent advise tenant companies. In addition, owners are involved to a lesser degree in other ways: 38 percent are paid full-time staff; 37 percent take an equity position with tenant companies for services rendered; 32 percent are passive investors in a financial pool; 27 percent are paid part-time consultants; and 21 percent serve as board members of tenant companies.

University Affiliation

Of the fifty incubators responding to the survey, 80.6 percent indicated some type of affiliation with a university. As shown in figure 5–5, one-third of the incubators maintain an informal organizational affiliation, and 25 percent maintain a formal organizational affiliation with a university. In addition, 23 percent indicated other ties to a university, which include having former university professors as managers or advisers and having university faculty entrepreneurs in the tenant companies.

Those claiming an affiliation with a university are also physically close to the university. As shown in figure 5–6, 39.4 percent are five to ten minutes from the university by car; 27.3 percent are within walking distance; 18.2 percent are ten to sixty minutes from the university by car; and 15.2 percent are actually on a university campus.

The Incubator Manager

The vast majority of incubator managers have no equity ownership in the incubator. Only 11.9 percent of the managers claimed equity ownership.

The ages of incubator managers range widely. As shown in figure 5–7, 20.6 percent are under thirty-one years old; 23.5 percent are thirty-one to

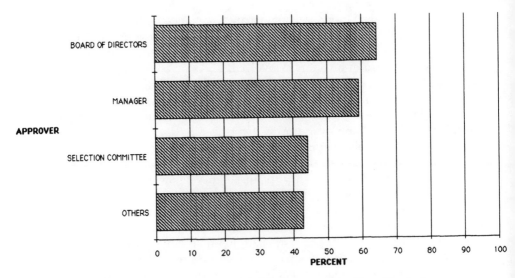

Figure 5–3. Who Gives Final Approval to New Tenants

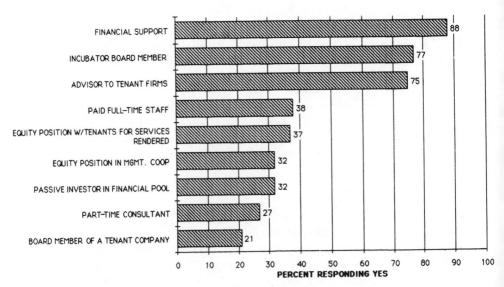

Figure 5–4. Owner's Involvement in Incubator

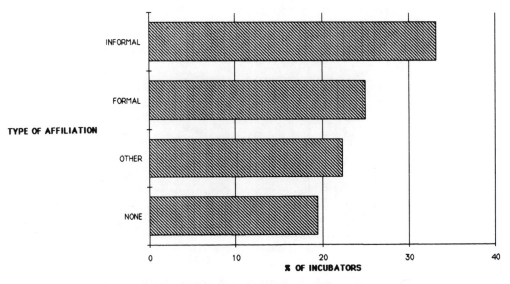

Figure 5–5. Incubator's Affiliation with a University

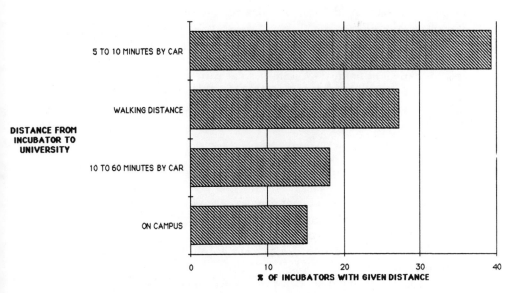

Figure 5–6. Incubator's Proximity to a University

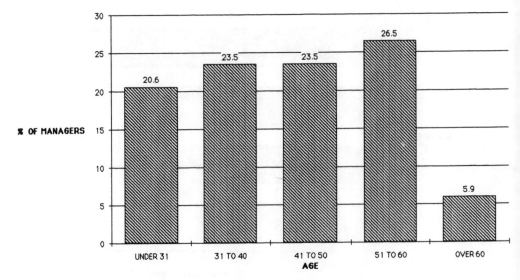

Figure 5–7. Incubator Manager's Age

forty; 23.5 percent are forty-one to fifty; 26.5 percent are fifty-one to sixty; and 5.9 percent are over sixty years old.

Figure 5–8 depicts the educational level of incubator managers. The majority, 54.3 percent, hold a bachelor's degree; 20 percent have a master's degree; 14.3 percent hold a doctoral degree; and only 11.4 percent indicated no college education.

Although salaries for incubator managers range from less than $20,000 to more than $70,000 per year, the majority of managers earn $29,000 or less. As shown in figure 5–9, 13.6 percent earn less than $20,000 per year; 40.9 percent make $20,000 to $29,000; 18.2 percent earn $30,000 to $39,000; 13.7 percent make $40,000 to $69,000; and 13.6 percent make $70,000 or more per year.

Building and Location

Most incubator buildings are not new. In fact, 54.5 percent of the incubators responding to the survey indicated that their buildings were over fifty years old. In addition, 40.1 percent of the incubators are in twenty-one- to fifty-year-old buildings, and only 5.8 percent are in buildings less than twenty years old.

Consequently, building renovations are usually required to meet the needs of new companies. In the survey, 40.7 percent of the incubators spent

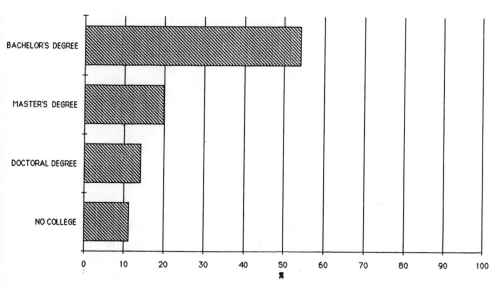

Figure 5–8. Incubator Manager's Level of Education

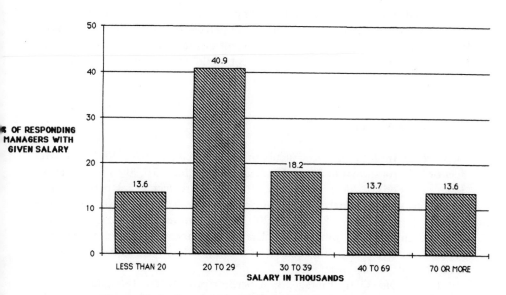

Figure 5–9. Incubator Manager's Annual Salary

over $500,000 on renovation; 37 percent spent $101,000 to $500,000; and 22.2 percent spent up to $100,000. Despite the costs required for renovation, only 9.1 percent of the responding incubators used historic site tax credits to help finance renovation, although 25.7 percent were eligible for the credits.

The planning period for the initial incubator site ranged from less than six months to over thirty-six months. The majority, 57.5 percent, took six to eighteen months to plan the incubator; 17.5 percent took less than six months; 15 percent took nineteen to twenty-four months; 7.5 percent took twenty-five to thirty-six months; and 2.5 percent took more than thirty-six months for the planning process (figure 5–10).

Most incubators that responded to the survey, 60.4 percent, are located in urban areas; 22.9 percent are in suburbs; and 16.7 percent are in rural locations.

It is interesting to find that incubators are in smaller rather than larger urban areas. As shown in figure 5–11, 44.6 percent of the incubators responding to the survey are in cities of 30,000 or fewer people; 16.9 percent are in cities of 31,000 to 100,000; 12.7 percent are in cities of 100,000 to 200,000; 16.8 percent are in cities of 200,000 to 1 million; and 8.4 percent are in cities with greater than 1 million population.

The responses to the survey also revealed other information about incubator facilities. As shown in figure 5–12, 80 percent of the responding incubators occupy renovated buildings; 70.6 percent indicated that their facilities are in industrial buildings; 64.9 percent said their facilities were in office buildings; 59.4 percent of the respondents lease their buildings; 51.9 percent are housed in larger commercial buildings; 50 percent of the incubators actually own the buildings they occupy; 39.3 percent occupy facilities that were newly built for the incubators; 34.6 percent of the incubators are sole occupants of their buildings; and 17.8 percent of the respondents previously occupied other facilities.

Lease Arrangements

In *total* square footage, most incubators (64.4 percent) have 40,000 square feet or less. As shown in figure 5–13, 20 percent have 10,000 square feet or less; 22.2 percent have 11,000 to 20,000 square feet; 22.2 percent have 21,000 to 40,000 square feet; 15.6 percent have 41,000 to 80,000 square feet; 11.1 percent have 81,000 to 200,000 square feet; and 8.9 percent are larger than 200,000 square feet. The total square footage of incubators ranges from a low of 2,000 square feet to a high of 500,000 square feet, with a median of 30,000 square feet.

In *leasable* square footage, 39.5 percent provide 20,000 square feet or less; 27.7 percent provide 21,000 to 50,000 square feet; 13.9 percent provide

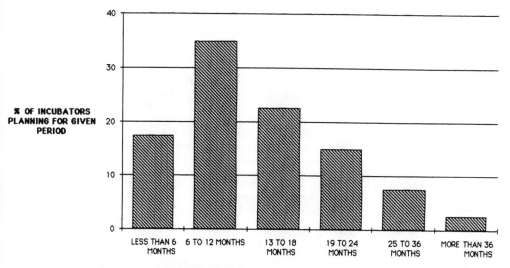

Figure 5–10. Planning Period for Initial Incubator Site

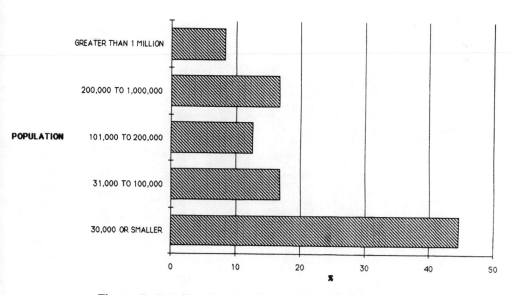

Figure 5–11. City Population at Incubator Location

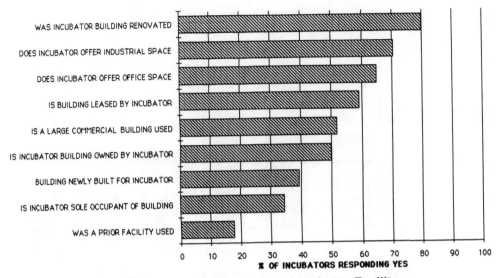

Figure 5–12. Questions about Incubator Facility

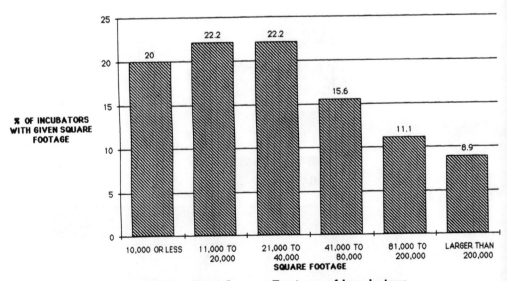

Figure 5–13. Total Square Footage of Incubators

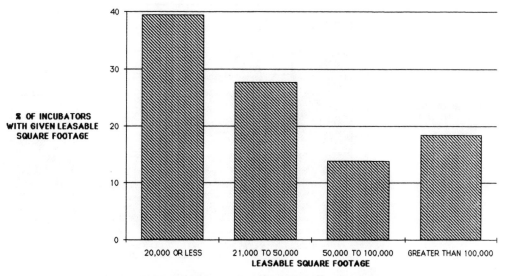

40

30

% OF INCUBATORS
WITH GIVEN LEASABLE   20
SQUARE FOOTAGE

10

0

20,000 OR LESS   21,000 TO 50,000   50,000 TO 100,000   GREATER THAN 100,000
LEASABLE SQUARE FOOTAGE

Figure 5–14. Incubator's Leasable Square Footage

51,000 to 100,000 square feet; and 18.4 percent have more than 100,000 leasable square feet (figure 5–14).

Currently leased square footage in the responding incubators is as follows: 63.2 percent of the incubators are currently leasing 20,000 square feet or less; 15.7 percent are leasing 21,000 to 50,000 square feet; 10.6 percent are leasing 51,000 to 100,000; and 10.5 percent are now leasing more than 100,000 square feet.

The average percentage of leased space varies by size of incubator. On the average, 60.5 percent of the facility is leased in incubators that have 20,000 square feet or less of leasable space; 51.1 percent in incubators of 21,000 to 50,000 square feet; 48.1 percent in incubators of 51,000 to 100,000 square feet; and 44.9 percent in incubators with 101,000 to 500,000 square feet.

Incubators usually provide four types of space to tenant companies. As shown in figure 5–15, 93.3 percent of responding incubators provide office space; 90.7 percent provide manufacturing space; 55 percent offer laboratory space; and 41 percent have warehouse space.

Average annual rental rates per square foot range from less than $2 to more than $10. As shown in figure 5–16, 29.2 percent of the responding incubators charge $2 or less per square foot; 39 percent charge from $3 to $5; 26.8 percent require $6 to $10; and 4.8 percent ask more than $10 per square foot. Of the respondents, 2.4 percent provide space free of charge, and the highest cost is $16 per square foot (from 2.4 percent of the respondents).

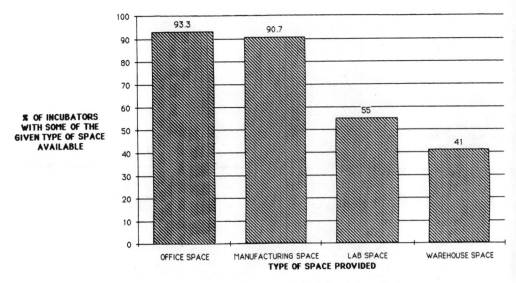

Figure 5–15. Types of Space Available at Incubators

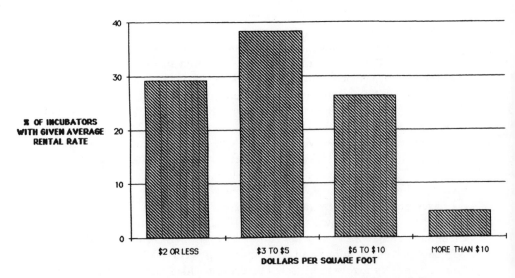

Figure 5–16. Average Annual Rental Rates per Square Foot

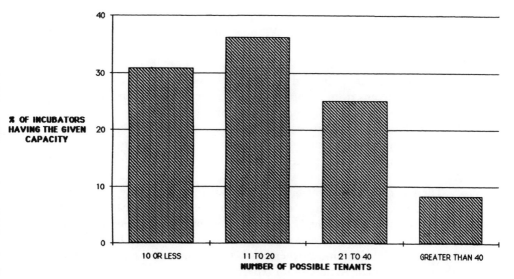

Figure 5–17. Incubator's Tenant Capacity

Most incubators estimated their tenant capacity at twenty firms or fewer. As shown in figure 5–17, 30.7 percent of the respondents have a capacity for ten or fewer tenant firms; 36.3 percent have a capacity for eleven to twenty firms; 24.2 percent have room for twenty-one to forty firms; and 8.4 percent can provide space for more than forty tenant companies.

The average square footage per tenant company varies. On the average, 45 percent of tenant firms occupy 1,000 square feet or less; 20 percent occupy 1,100 to 2,000 square feet; 17.5 percent occupy 2,100 to 4,000 square feet; and 17.5 percent occupy more than 4,000 square feet.

The majority of leases have flexible terms. Of the responding incubators, 69.2 percent offer flexible terms, and 30.8 require some sort of fixed lease arrangement. These flexible arrangements are reflected in the average length of the tenant lease. In 12.1 percent of the incubators, the average length of the tenant lease is less than twelve months, with a range of one, two, three, and six months in duration; in 46.3 percent of the incubators, the average length of the tenant lease is twelve months; in 19.5 percent, thirteen to twenty-four months; and in 21.9 percent, the average lease is twenty-five or more months.

Sources of Financial Support

Financial support for incubators comes from a variety of sources, including the community, state government, and the federal government.

In community-related assistance, incubators have received financial assistance from a range of sources. As shown in figure 5–18, 69 percent of the responding incubators received financial support from private sources; 62.5 percent from city government; 55.6 percent from other local sources; 38.1 percent from private industrial councils; 37.5 percent from county government; 36.8 percent from a university; 33.3 percent from chambers of commerce; and 7.1 percent from industrial revenue bonds.

In addition, 63 percent of the incubators responding receive financial assistance from state agencies; 44.4 percent received support from other state authorities; and 25 percent received aid from state revolving funds (figure 5–19).

The federal government has also provided job assistance. As shown in figure 5–20, of the incubators responding to the survey, 60 percent received financial assistance from the Economic Development Administration (EDA); 55 percent from a Community Development Block Grant (CDBG); 38.9 percent from the Job Training Partnership Act (JTPA); and 17.6 percent from an Urban Development Action Grant (UDAG).

Operating Expenses

For incubators responding to the survey, annual operating budgets ranged from a low of $35,000 to a high of over $1 million, with a median of $110,000. As shown in figure 5–21, 40 percent of the incubators have annual budgets in the $50,000 to $100,000 range. The next largest budget category, 22.8 percent, is the $101,000 to $150,000 range.

Expenses are presented in three ways: average annual expenses, median annual expenses, and ranges within each expense category. Average annual expenses are shown in figure 5–22. Highest average annual expenses are as follows: $43,800 for overhead; $27,900 for maintenance; $24,900 for rent or lease of incubator building; $18,400 for building and grounds maintenance; $16,400 for equipment purchases; and $14,400 for consultants.

The picture is somewhat different when median annual expenses are considered. As shown in figure 5–23, overhead is still highest, at $25,000. The next highest median annual expense is consultants, at $14,500, followed by rent or lease of $11,500, maintenance of $10,300, building and grounds maintenance of $7,500, and equipment purchases of $5,000.

Annual overhead expenses ranged from a low of nothing to over $1 million. Of the responding incubators, 44.4 percent had annual overhead expenses of $20,000 or less, and 27.8 percent had more than $95,000 in annual overhead expenses. Annual maintenance costs ranged from a low of $1,000 to a high of $173,000. Most of the responding incubators (51.7 percent) had

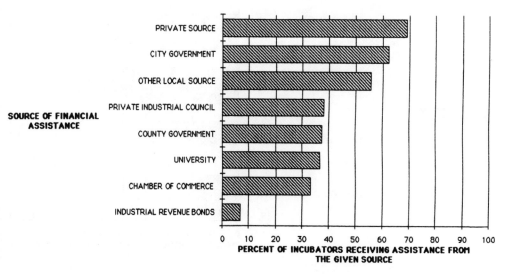

Figure 5–18. Community-Related Sources of Incubator
Financial Support

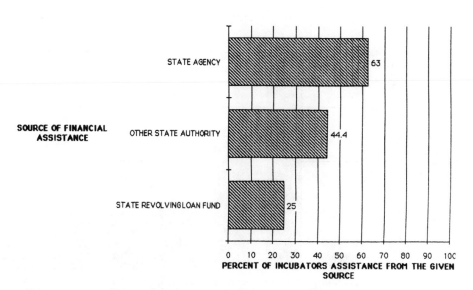

Figure 5–19. State Government Sources of Incubator
Financial Support

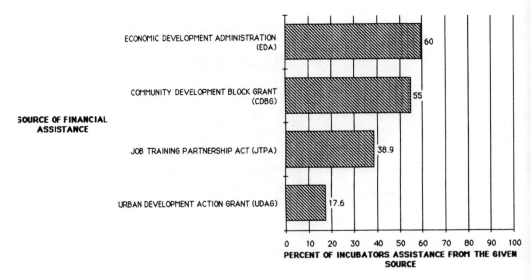

Figure 5–20. Federal Government Sources of Incubator
Financial Support

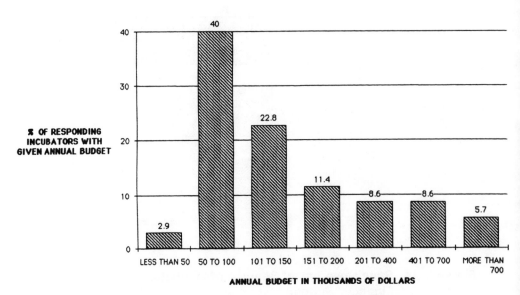

Figure 5–21. Incubator Annual Operating Budget

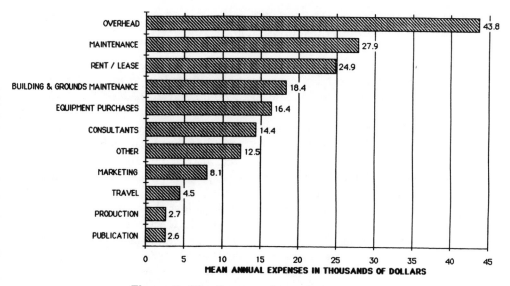

Figure 5–22. Average Annual Expenses

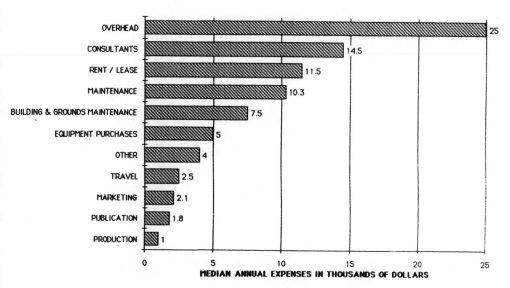

Figure 5–23. Median Annual Expenses

annual maintenance costs of $10,000 or less, and 34.5 percent had annual maintenance costs of $11,000 to $50,000.

Annual rent or lease expenses ranged from a low of nothing to a high of over $100,000. Of the responding incubators, 45 percent paid less than $10,000 in annual rent or lease expenses; 30 percent paid $10,000 to $29,000; 15 percent paid $30,000 to $99,000; and 10 percent paid more than $99,000.

Annual building and grounds maintenance expense ranged from a low of nothing to over $100,000: 40.9 percent had $5,000 or less in buildings or grounds maintenance expense; 22.7 percent had $6,000 to $10,000; 13.7 percent had $11,000 to $30,000; 13.6 percent had $31,000 to $50,000; and 9 percent had $51,000 or more.

Annual equipment purchases ranged from a low of $1,000 to a high of over $100,000. Of the responding incubators, 47.1 percent purchased less than $5,000 worth of equipment annually; 23.5 percent purchased $5,000 to $19,000; 11.8 percent purchased $20,000 to $29,000; 11.7 percent purchased $30,000 to $99,000; and 5.9 percent purchased over $99,000 worth of equipment.

Annual consultant expenses ranged from nothing to a high of $35,000: 28.6 percent of responding incubators paid less than $5,000 for consultants annually; 35.7 percent paid $5,000 to $19,000; 21.4 percent paid $20,000 to $29,000 and 14.3 percent paid over $30,000.

Other annual expenses ranged from a low of $1,000 to over $100,000. The large majority of responding incubators, 76.9 percent, paid $5,000 or less for other expenses.

Annual marketing expenses ranged from a low of $1,000 to a high of $100,000. The large majority of incubators, 83.3 percent, had annual marketing expenses of $5,000 or less.

Annual travel expenses ranged from zero to a high of $26,000. The large majority of incubators, 86.4 percent, paid less than $5,000 for annual travel expenses.

Annual publication expenses ranged from a low of $1,000 to a high of $8,000. 40 percent of responding incubators had $1,000 or less in annual publication expenses; 30 percent had $2,000; 15 percent had $3,000 to $5,000; and 15 percent had over $6,000.

Salaries

Employee compensation in incubators includes executive, administrative, and support salaries. Salary structures vary considerably, depending on the scope, purpose, and location of the incubator.

Total incubator salaries ranged from a low of $12,000 to a high of

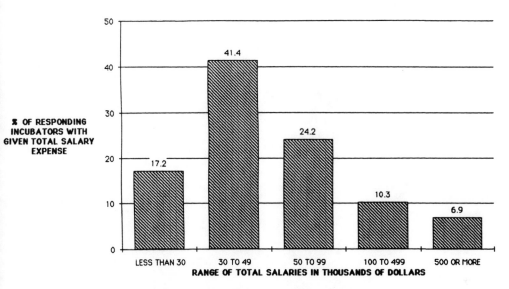

**% OF RESPONDING
INCUBATORS WITH
GIVEN TOTAL SALARY
EXPENSE**

RANGE OF TOTAL SALARIES IN THOUSANDS OF DOLLARS

Figure 5–24. Total Incubator Salaries

$922,000, with a median of $45,000. As shown in figure 5–24, 41.4 percent of responding incubators had $30,000 to $49,000 in total annual salaries; 24.2 percent had $50,000 to $99,000; 17.2 percent had less than $30,000; 10.3 percent had $100,000 to $499,000; and 6.9 percent had $500,000 or more in total annual salaries.

Executive salaries ranged from a low of $2,000 to a high of over $100,000, with a median of $29,000. Of the responding incubators, 47.6 percent provided $25,000 to $50,000 in executive salaries; 38.1 percent provided less than $25,000; and 14.3 percent provided more than $50,000.

Administrative salaries ranged from nothing to a high of over $99,000. Of the responding incubators, 64 percent provided $20,000 or less in administrative salaries; 27 percent provided $21,000 to $99,000; and 9 percent provided more than $99,000.

Support salaries ranged from a low of $1,000 to a high of $30,000. Most responding incubators, 55 percent, provided less than $15,000 in support salaries; 35 percent provided $18,000 to $20,000; and 10 percent provided more than $20,000.

6
Selection and Management

Objectives

Incubator manager and directors were asked to list their top three objectives in starting the incubator. By far, the number one objective was to create new jobs; 66.7 percent responded that this was the first goal of the incubator. To promote economic development was the primary objective of 13.3 percent of the respondents, and to make a profit was first for 8.9 percent (figure 6–1).

When the top three objectives are taken collectively, job creation still ranks first, with a 81 percent response; economic development received a 69.1 percent response; and entrepreneurship development had a 47.3 percent response (figure 6–2).

Relation to Tenant Companies

Incubators have established clear preferences for the types of companies that they would like in their incubators. When respondents were asked their first choice of tenants, by industry type, over 40 percent indicated light manufacturing and high-technology. When the top three choices are taken collectively, 85.7 percent indicated a preference for high-technology, and 80 percent favored light manufacturing (figure 6–3). Incubator owners or sponsors and managers are making a link between their objectives of job creation, economic development, and entrepreneurship development and the high-technology and light manufacturing industries.

Incubators have also established a set of criteria for tenant selection. Figure 6–4 shows what respondents indicated as the most important criteria for tenant company selection. Nearly 80 percent look for companies that will create new jobs; over 60 percent require that companies pay their own operating costs; and 50 percent require a written business plan. In addition, 35 percent of the respondents favor firms that appear to have a unique opportunity; 35 percent require that the firm be a new, start-up enterprise; and

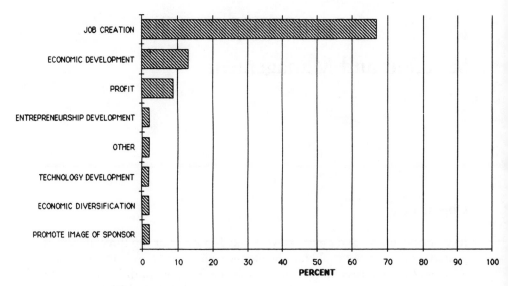

Figure 6–1. Incubator's Number One Objective

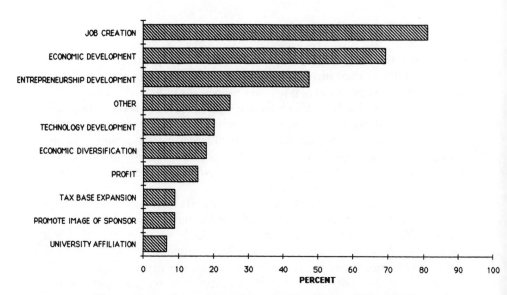

Figure 6–2. One of Incubator's Top Three Objectives

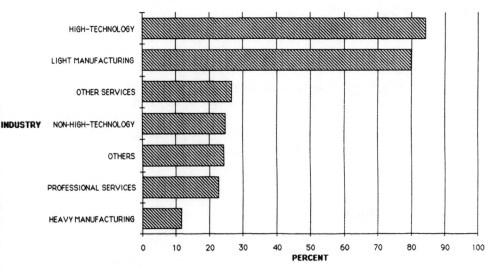

Figure 6–3. One of Incubator's Three Top Choices for Tenants' Industry Type

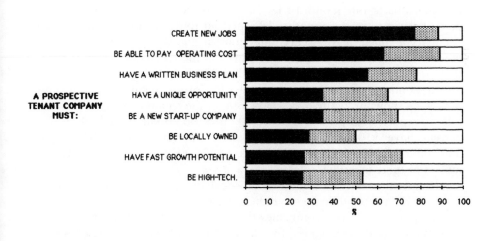

☐ LOW IMPORTANCE   ▧ MEDIUM IMPORTANCE   ■ VERY IMPORTANT

Figure 6–4. Importance of Selected Criteria in Tenant Selection

over 25 percent look for fast growth potential. When the *most important criteria* is added to the *important criteria* response, creating new jobs and paying operation cost rank highest, followed by written business plan, fast growth potential, new start-up, and unique opportunity.

As shown in figure 6–5, the least important criteria were ranked in the following order: 90 percent are not interested in expert references; over 70 percent do not seek equity in the companies; 65 percent are not interested in a company with a proprietary product; nearly 60 percent do not require companies to be in a specific industry; and nearly 60 percent do not think it is important for a company to meet low-income requirements.

Tenant Companies

The survey developed data from tenant companies on number of employees, months in incubator, annual sales, duration of tenancy, and company location after graduation.

Respondents to the survey reported the number of employees for 211 tenant companies. As shown in figure 6–6, 42.2 percent of the tenant companies had one or two employees; 80.1 percent had ten employees or fewer; 13.3 percent had eleven to thirteen employees, and 6.6 percent had thirty-one employees or more.

Respondents reported on the number of months that 188 current tenants have been in the incubators. Figure 6–7 indicates that 13.8 percent had been in the incubator one month or less; 27.1 percent two to six months; 27.1 percent seven to twelve months; 19.7 percent thirteen to eighteen months; 8.5 percent nineteen to twenty-four months; and 3.7 percent twenty-five months or more. The relatively brief times in the incubator reflect the fact that the majority of incubators are themselves relatively new.

Respondents reported on annual sales for forty-two current tenant companies. As shown in figure 6–8, 7.3 percent of the tenant companies have no sales to report; 29.3 percent have $1,000 to $100,000 in annual sales; 17.1 percent have $101,000 to $200,000; 14.6 percent have $201,000 to $400,000; 9.8 percent have $401,000 to $999,000; and 22 percent have $1 million or more in annual sales.

Despite the relative newness of the incubator concept, some companies have already started to leave or graduate from their facilities. Survey respondents reported on thirty companies that had graduated. Figure 6–9 shows that of these thirty companies, five, or 16 percent, have left in less than six months; four or 13.3 percent in six to eleven months; six or 20 percent in twelve to seventeen months; seven or 23.3 percent in eighteen to twenty-three months; one or 3.3 percent in twenty-four to thirty-five months; three or 10

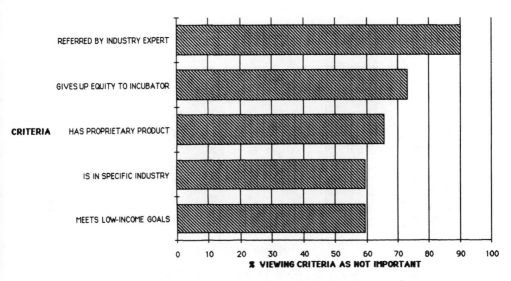

Figure 6–5. The Six Least Important Criteria for Tenant Selection

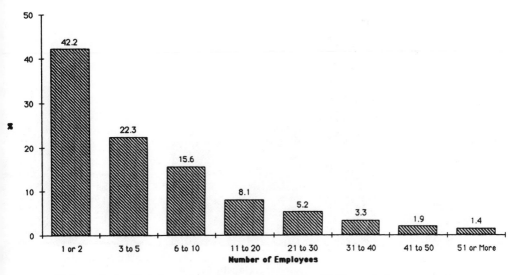

Figure 6–6. Number of Employees at Current Tenant Companies

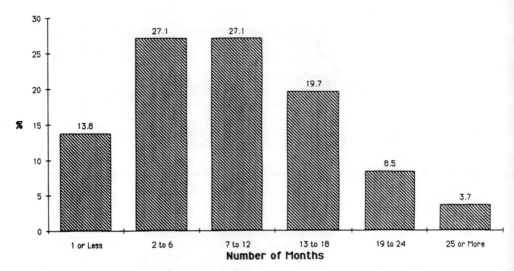

Figure 6–7. Number of Months That Current Tenants Have Been
in Incubator

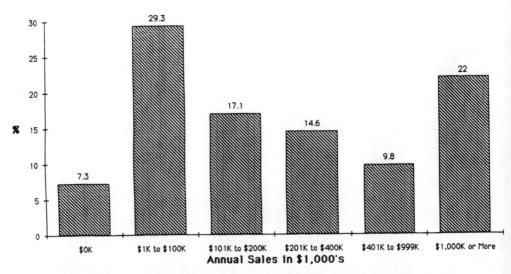

Figure 6–8. Annual Sales of Current Tenant Companies

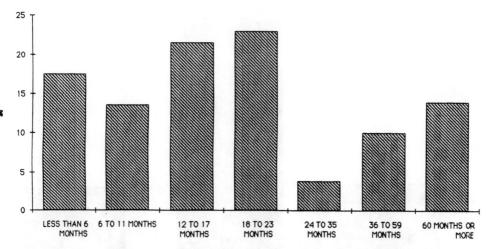

Figure 6–9. Number of Months That Graduated Company Was in Incubator

percent in thirty-six to fifty-nine months; and four or 13 percent have left after five years or more in the incubator.

Figure 6–10 shows that incubators do seem to contribute to building indigenous companies. Of the graduate firms, 20 percent stayed in the same neighborhood as the incubator; 60 percent remained in the same city, and 20 percent stayed in the same state.

Incubator Services

Incubators provide a range of services for tenant companies. Services can be grouped into four categories; secretarial, administrative, consulting, and facilities.

Figure 6–11 shows the percentage of respondents providing secretarial services:

Word processing	90.7%
Typing	88.9%
Photocopying	86.7%
Receptionist duties	79.1%
Clerical	72.1%
Filing	45.0%

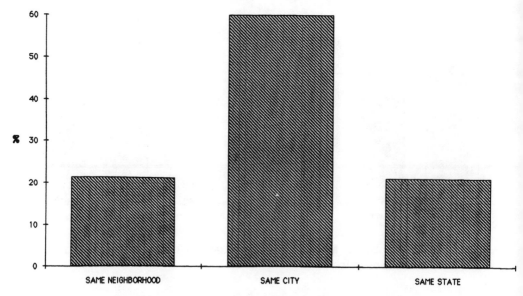

Figure 6–10. Company Location after Graduation

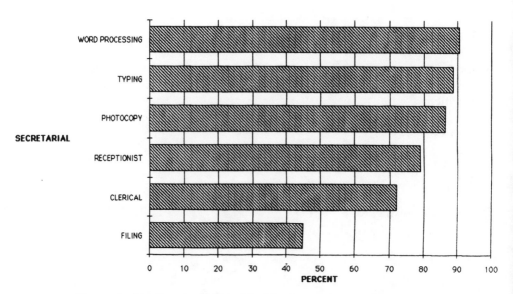

Figure 6–11. Services Provided by Incubators—Secretarial

Figure 6–12 shows the percentage of respondents providing administrative services:

Mailing	70.7%
Accounting	61.5%
Equipment rental	56.3%
Billing	53.7%
Contract administration	50.0%
Health insurance	33.3%

Figure 6–13 shows the percentage of respondents providing consulting services:

General counseling	93.0%
Marketing	86.0%
Loan packaging	79.5%
Accounting	75.0%
Legal	66.7%
Introduction to venture capitalists	61.8%
Financial contracts	59.5%
Head hunting	41.5%

Figure 6–14 shows the percentage of respondents providing various types of facilities:

Security	90.7%
Conference room	90.7%
Other	85.7%
Computers	75.0%
Library	72.1%
Loading docks	60.5%
Laboratory	41.7%
Exhibition space	33.3%
Day care	7.9%

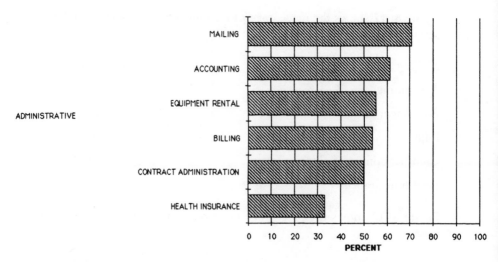

Figure 6–12. Services Provided by Incubators—Administrative

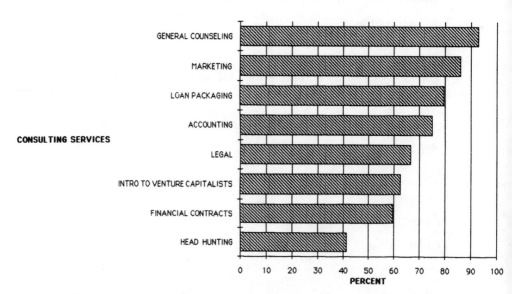

Figure 6–13. Services Provided by Incubators—Consulting

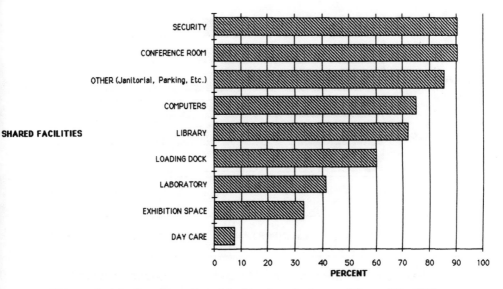

SHARED FACILITIES

Figure 6–14. Services Provided by Incubators—Shared Facilities

The survey also asked respondents to evaluate the relative importance to tenant companies of each of the services provided. Their responses are presented in terms of *most important, important,* and *least important* services.

Figure 6–15 shows the percentage of respondents rating specific secretarial services. The *most important* services, in order of priority, are as follows:

Photocopying	57.5%
Receptionist duties	57.1%
Word processing	38.4%
Typing	32.5%
Clerical	25.0%
Filing	7.4%

When *important* responses are also considered, photocopying and receptionist duties still rank highest, followed by clerical, typing, and word processing.

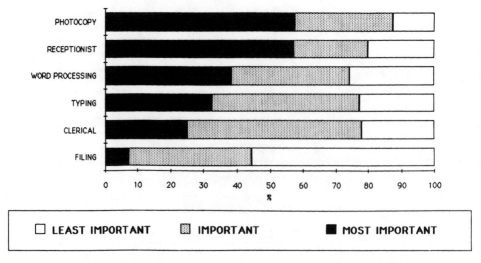

Figure 6–15. Importance of Secretarial Services Provided

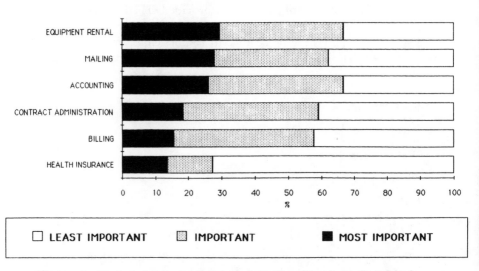

Figure 6–16. Importance of Administrative Services Provided

Figure 6–16 shows the percentage of respondents rating specific administrative services. The *most important* services in order of priority are as follows:

Equipment rental	29.2%
Mailing	27.6%
Accounting	25.9%
Contract administration	18.2%
Billing	15.4%
Health insurance	13.6%

When *important* responses are also considered, equipment rental still ranks highest, along with accounting, followed by mailing, contract administration, and billing.

Figure 6–17 shows the percentage of respondents rating specific consulting services. The *most important* services, in order of priority, are as follows:

Business planning	62.5%
Marketing	61.6%
Accounting	60.6%
Managerial	60.6%
Evaluating financial options	57.5%
Access to grants & loans	55.6%
General counseling	51.4%
Loan packaging	50.0%
Introduction to venture capitalist	50.0%

Other consulting services were rated *most important* as follows: technical, 42.4 percent; legal, 40.7 percent; tax planning, 32.3 percent; head hunting, 11.1 percent. When *important* responses are also considered managerial ranks highest, with marketing and evaluating financial options next, followed by business planning, accounting, general counseling, and access to grants and loans. Loan packaging and introduction to venture capitalists also rank very high.

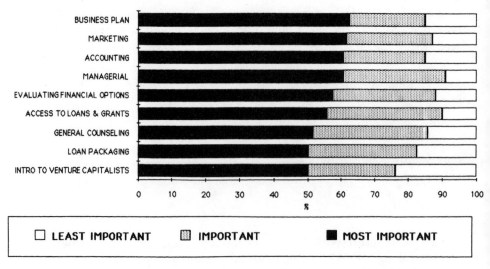

Figure 6–17. Importance of Consulting Services Provided

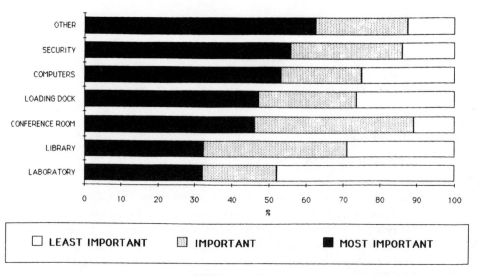

Figure 6–18. Importance of Shared Facilities Provided

Figure 6–18 shows the percentage of respondents rating specific facilities services. The *most important* services, in order of priority are as follows:

Other	62.5%
Security	55.5%
Computers	53.2%
Loading dock	47.1%
Conference room	45.9%
Laboratory	32.3%
Library	32.3%

Other facilities services were rated *most important* as follows: exhibition space, 12.5 percent; day care, 5.6 percent.

When *important* responses are also considered, conference room ranks highest, followed by other, security, computers, loading dock, library, and laboratory.

7
Case Studies
of New Business Incubators

This chapter presents case studies of four types of incubator models:

university-related;

community sponsored;

corporate/franchise; and

private.

As shown by these case studies, no two incubators are exactly alike. Despite apparent similarities in sponsorship, each incubator develops a unique personality. This personality may be defined by a variety of variables, such as goals, operational guidelines, environmental variables, and funding. Each incubator's personality is determined not only by these variables, but also by the set of circumstances that surround its initial development.

In many instances, the unique character of an incubator is determined by the personality of the management team. This is true because the establishment of an incubator is often as entrepreneurial an effort as the building of, for instance, a new high-technology company. Such a company may initiate its operations with definitive plans and goals that change dramatically due to market conditions and other constraints. The incubators chronicled in this section have all evolved from their initial incubator concept. One example of the entrepreneurship required of incubator founders and managers is the variety of approaches taken to secure space for the incubators: Rubicon, a private incubator, rents the space it requires for its companies from commercial brokers; Control Data purchased and completely renovated a building for its first incubator; Rensselaer Polytechnic Institute first housed its incubator in some underutilized classrooms until permanent space—a renovated building formerly used as home for wayward girls—was available; the Fullton-Carroll Center purchased an abandoned building and rennovated only as much as was absolutely necessary for occupancy due to budgetary constraints; and the Advanced Technology Development Center used an abandoned high school until it could build new buildings.

Other constraints faced by each incubator impact the philosophy of its organization. The Fullton-Carroll Center, for example, allows very large tenants because it has a huge facility to rent. Rubicon, on the other hand, will never have more than one tenth of the space of the Fullton-Carroll Center because the amount of money and time it invests in each client company limits its ability to handle many companies. Even among incubators of similar models, there are large differences between their operations and goals. For example, although the Advanced Technology Development Center and the Rensselaer Polytechnic Institute are university-based incubators, each has a different orientation. RPI is endeavoring to build an environment which will add diversity and dynanism to the rest of the university. The ATDC is oriented toward developing the high-technology resources of Georgia, and receives significant yearly funding from the state legislature to do so.

As a result of the variables which make each incubator different, there may be no one ideal incubator model, and an individual incubator model may not be transferable in its entirety to another area. Nevertheless, there is much to be learned from the experiences of some of the pioneers of the still fledgling incubator industry.

This chapter presents six case studies of some of the pioneering incubators in the industry. While each of these incubators shares a common, fundamental goal, namely, to increase the ease, efficiency and staying power of the new business start-up, each has distinct mechanisms by which it intends to achieve this goal. When reading the following case studies, it is useful to keep in mind that each of these incubators was started without the prior knowledge of the mechanisms of other incubators. In a sense, the people who initiated these incubators did not set out to create an incubator per se, since they knew of no organizational model which would help accomplish their goals, or because they did not know that what they were to develop would turn out to be an incubator. Yet, what they have created provides the conceptual foundations for the rest of the incubator industry.

University-Related:

Rensselaer Polytechnic Institute

High on a hill overlooking the banks of the Hudson River, the stately campus of Rensselaer Polytechnic Institute (RPI), since 1824, has lent an air of stability and intellect to the city of Troy, in upper New York state. A private university, RPI has long been a crown jewel in that section of the prosperous Hudson River Valley, a region known historically for its industrial strength. During the past quarter of a century, however, this industrial strength has been eroded and jobs have been lost to technological obsolescence, to foreign competition, or to migrations to other states. RPI's graduates, a major resource of the region, have also been migrating to other regions in search of employment. By 1976, the emerging centers of new industrialization had passed by the Capital District of New York and had become firmly entrenched in Northern California, Massachusetts, and North Carolina.

On the surface, this uneventful and inexorable process affected RPI little, since the school was, and still is, known as a first-class technical institution whose reputation is national, not just regional. But in the late 1970s, the microelectronics revolution was just beginning, and competition for quality professors, researchers, and instructors was heating up as industry fought with academia for the finest minds available. Often the salary offered by a position was not the deciding factor for where a top professor would choose to work; instead his choice was frequently determined by such factors as quality of life, consulting opportunities, graduate program quality, and the momentum of research programs. Not only was it increasingly difficult for quality engineering schools to recruit outstanding professors, but it was also increasingly difficult to attract top-quality graduate students, who were either highly employable by high-technology firms or were lured to big-name schools with large endowments and highly visible research programs. With its frost-belt climate and decaying industrial base, the school's location in Troy had become a significant negative variable in the effort to lure top-flight faculty to RPI.

In 1976, George M. Low became the fourteenth president of RPI. Low's previous position was deputy administrator of the National Aeronautics and

Space Administration, the agency's number-two executive position, in which he was manager of the Apollo moonshot project. One of the first initiatives Low undertook was the development of a strategic planning document to determine where the university should be by the year 2000. This study, titled "Rensselaer 2000," observed that RPI had such notable attributes as an outstanding undergraduate program, a national reputation, a healthy endowment (approaching $125 million), and well-placed alumni. The study concluded that one of the top priorities for RPI should be the establishment of a graduate program.

In science-based subjects, the most expeditious way to establish a reputation as a top-flight school is to have highly visible research programs that are in the forefront of current theory. To accomplish this, it is necessary to attract the top minds in a field, the stars of a discipline, to a graduate program so that it may become recognized quickly. At RPI, these top researchers are referred to as "steeples of excellence," because they shine bright, can be seen above the multitudes from a distance, and possess qualities that attract other top researchers. Such professors, because they also attract the top graduate students, serve not only as the initiating variables of a prestigious graduate program but also as a focal point for the elements that comprise a top-quality program.

In 1979, the major obstacle to Rensselaer 2000's suggested graduate program was the ability of the school to attract first-rate researchers. Without consulting opportunities for the professors or part-time work in industry for graduate students, the availability of research talent was very limited. To fight this obstacle, the school's administration decided to take the lead in developing the area for technical growth.

Many years before, RPI had been given 1,200 acres of land not far from Troy. The school had briefly considered relocating the campus to this land in the 1950s, but no real improvements had yet been made on the property. It was suggested that this land become a research or industrial park, since this would serve the dual purpose of attracting high-technology firms to the area and, in addition, providing income from a relatively untapped resource. At about the same time, President Low discovered during a trip to Silicon Valley that Stanford University had received substantial financial support by providing laboratory space to the founders of Hewlett-Packard. He believed strongly that this type of alliance was a tactic RPI should employ, one that had the potential for monetary and ancillary benefits to the university. In 1979, the university appointed a task force to study the feasibility of developing a technology park. The task force recommended that the university should proceed on a smaller scale—to discern if, in fact, high technology could flourish in the area—before it made a large-scale financial commitment to develop such a technical park.

Through this process, the seed for an incubator spontaneously germinated at a time when the word *incubator* had not yet been used in connection with business development. The RPI incubator was to be a place where technically oriented people wishing to start a business could do so with the aid and resources of a technical university.

Because the RPI incubator was initiated when the concept had not been tested, the university had no model to follow. To develop the concept, a working committee was formed. This committee was headed by James E. Morley, vice-president for finance and administration. Other committee members were Michael Wacholder, an urban planner in RPI's Urban and Environment Studies Program; Raymond A. Lancaster, treasurer of RPI; Dr. Pier Abetti, professor in the School of Management; and Jerome T. Mahone, then the university investment officer, with responsibility for the endowment portfolio. Jerry Mahone was the program's first full-time director and still runs the incubator. The working committee was designed to involve a wide variety of thought from the university's various disciplines and to represent a cross section of the university's interests. Taking its lead from the university's technical orientation, the committee determined that the incubator unit would cater only to technically oriented companies.

The incubator unit was initially set up in the basement of a classroom building while a permanent facility, an empty classroom building, was being renovated. The empty classroom building, which had been part of the holdings of a convent before the university acquired it—the incubator building had been a home for wayward girls, and the former nunnery now houses the university's computer center—was renovated with $700,000 from the proceeds of industrial revenue bonds and $200,000 from the New York State Urban Development Corporation. The amortization schedule for these two debt instruments deferred payments during the first five years to allow a period of cash flow from the developing program.

Initially, the incubator's tenant companies were attracted by word of mouth, and entrepreneurs setting up companies were either university affiliated, technology-company affiliated, or extant technology companies with the need for inexpensive space and technical staffs. These three sources of entrepreneurs are still the mainstay of the RPI incubator program. The number of companies in the incubator depended on the size of the available facility, and the program grew rapidly. The incubator was managed by the working committee for the first three years, during which time there was also a part-time director.

In June 1983, Jerry Mahone assumed the position of director. At the same time, the working committee was replaced with an advisory committee. The advisory committee is more broadly based than the working committee; it is composed of an academic administrator, a faculty member, an administration representative, a local businessperson, a national businessperson who has grown a small company, and a nationally recognized venture capitalist.

In its early phases, the program established ad hoc procedures for the incubator's administration. These procedures included such factors as how to evaluate the companies for admission to the incubator, how to judge the proper duration of residency for an incubator company, how to encourage a tenant company to leave, how to create and grow a stable revenue stream from the program, how to formalize interactions with the university community, and how to develop potential investment opportunities for possible participation in the university's endowment portfolio. It was intended that the advisory committee would formalize the procedures for dealing with these issues.

The evolution of the incubator's procedures began in the goals set by the university for the incubator. Jerry Mahone lists his goals for the incubator, with their relative priorities, as follows. His first priority is to establish an environment within the incubator that is conducive to and consistent with the environment and goals of the university as a whole. This signifies that the incubator will provide consulting opportunities for faculty, work opportunities for students—especially for graduate students—and, on the whole, will be a dynamic organization of which a world-class university would be proud. In addition, it signifies an environment that encourages the interaction of industry—inside the incubator or out—with RPI's academic community. Second, the incubator must be self-sufficient and not erode other university resources. Third, the incubator should provide investment opportunities for the university's endowment. Fourth, a goal for the incubator in particular and the university in general is to provide development opportunities for the Capital District of New York. Finally, the incubator should provide potential tenants for RPI's technology park. It seems likely that the first two priorities, establishing the environment and self-sufficiency, will be the primary factors on which the success of the incubator will be judged. Profit itself is a secondary issue, although it certainly remains a desirable goal.

An important feature of the RPI incubator program is that its development has been entirely evolutionary. This is partly because RPI has one of the oldest incubator programs in the country and therefore has had time to make more changes than have newer programs. But another aspect of its development is that the program was initiated without any comparable role models to follow and therefore has not been constrained by any preconceptions—true or false—of how the program should evolve. The program has had to justify each action according to its own goals and limitations. From this process, RPI has constructed an imaginative program, different from others in the country in its match of priorities and goals. This process is still evolving and still changing.

Currently, a prospective company must submit a business plan as the first step in the admission process. This filters out four out of every five prospective entrepreneurs. There are several reasons why RPI requires a business plan. The first is to make sure that the entrepreneur has actually thought through the project. The business plan separates those people who are infatuated with the idea of entrepreneurship from those people who are actually serious about the project and who understand the rigors necessary to build a business. In some cases, particularly with very technical enterprises, a business plan also serves as a gauge of the entrepreneur's sense of the prospective market. Mahone has found that an incubator must, at the earliest opportunity, instill in the prospective entrepreneur the need to understand the marketplace and whether it will accept the particular product or service. Often the requirement of a business plan serves to filter out those who are unwilling or unable to put in the work necessary to build a business. The requirements of a business plan are relatively simple: product description, market requirements, market size, financing required, background information on the principals of the company, and potential financial return to an investor.

The second requirement of the RPI incubator program is for the prospective company to demonstrate a technology currently being researched on the RPI campus. This is necessary because the first priority of the incubator program is to create an environment within the university that is conducive to technology, entrepreneurship, creativity, and the development of a world-class university. The incubator's success will be defined, to a degree, by its ability to develop formal links between the incubator program and the campus. The incubator will serve as a laboratory to help solve academic research questions. Mahone observes: "The most important thing is creating an environment, such that we attract the best and brightest to upstate New York, within financial limitations."

The third and final filter is what Jerry Mahone characterizes as a "sanity test"—a long discussion between him and the prospective entrepreneur. During this talk, Mahone attempts to judge whether the applicant understands the process of building a company and whether he is capable of the task. Mahone says that he is looking "for driven people, who won't be overwhelmed when they find out how deep the water is, and will be able to swim after they get over the initial trauma."

Although these filters define the admissions process, there are other criteria that the incubator would prefer to have in its tenant companies. For example, Mahone would prefer that tenant companies be in an advanced product-development stage. He would prefer that the companies hire students for their staff, that they use faculty as consultants, that they use university facilities (that is, lab space), and that they demonstrate significant entrepreneurial potential. There should also be a certain amount of synergy between the tenant company's technology and the technical expertise that RPI can offer. RPI has state-of-the-art technical programs in many fields, among which are interactive computer graphics, CAD/CAM, integrated electronics, robotics, automation and manufacturing productivity, biomedical engineering, microbiology, tribology and wear control, composite materials, power systems engineering, and chemical process design.

Once accepted into the incubator, tenant companies must give 2 percent of their company's equity to the incubator and must pay rent to the incubator as well. The amount of rent payable to the incubator depends on the status of the company when it enters the incubator: $6 per square foot for start-up companies and $8 per square foot for existing companies. All utilities are included in the rent. (Second-floor warehouse space in downtown Troy—a half mile distant—costs $3 per square foot, and office space in downtown Albany—twenty-five miles away—costs $15 per square foot.) Tenant companies also have access to various services offered by the incubator. These services include secretarial support, telephone answering, executive search, photocopying, consulting, and access to university laboratories, libraries, and computer facilities. All services are offered on a pay-as-you-go basis.

As of August 1985, there were twelve companies in the incubator and, for the first time, the incubator unit had empty space. Seven of these companies were start-ups and five were existing companies. The incubator has 30,000 square feet of office space and has room for about fifteen companies at a time. Twenty-five companies have been through the incubator, and four have ceased operations. Four companies have received venture capital; one company put together a research and development limited partnership; two companies raised money through private placement; and one company went public on a penny-stock exchange in Oklahoma.

It was somewhat embarrassing that the first company to leave the incubator moved to the Boston area, but RPI officials point out that the move was inspired by venture capital financing and did not have anything to do with the Capital District environment. The rest of the companies that have graduated RPI have stayed in the area. Most of these companies are still small, with fifteen to twenty-five employees. Mahone describes them as healthy infants. Companies are encouraged to leave the incubator by a variety of forces, both from within the company and from the incubator. Most companies have come and gone within twelve to eighteen months, having left because their needs had outgrown the space the incubator facility could provide. But the incubator also charges higher rent to companies that have been in residence for longer than two years. Although there is some flexibility, the incubator will also ask a company to leave if it cannot pay its rent on a consistent basis.

Participants in RPI's incubator see themselves being rewarded in several ways. First, association with RPI's incubator gives their company great credibility within the business community. One example of this is the story of an entrepreneur who left the incubator, yet paid $50 per month just to have his company's name left on the marquee. Another benefit of being associated with the incubator is the fact that companies have access to the RPI library facilities and immediate access to RPI's faculty. Although there is often a charge for this consulting arrangement, members of the faculty are often willing to be available for quick advice on either a business or a technical question. Jerry Mahone notices changes in his tenant companies as well. He observes that companies are more marketable for having been in the incubator. Entrepreneurs have been forced to look at business at a different level, to function on a different level. Their personal objectives change, says Mahone; their character and orientation become far more focused on business. All this creates a broader perspective among the incubator's graduated entrepreneurs.

RPI has initiated an associates program whereby entrepreneurs pay $1,000 per year to use some of the incubator's facilities but have their companies located elsewhere. Associate companies have access to university facilities and participate in breakfast meetings with incubator tenants. In the future, Mahone would like to make the incubator attractive to corporations, to locate intrapreneurship projects at the incubator rather than at corporate facilities. It is hoped that such projects would provide job opportunities for graduate students. In addition, he would like to diversify the range of technologies presently being pursued by tenant companies. Mahone foresees the eventual need for a seed-capital fund to be directly affiliated with the incubator. He would like to see this fund capitalized at around $5 million. Finally, it is possible that the incubator could become a public company on its own if it is able to establish a stabilized revenue stream that could support a stock price. This would enable the university to realize a capital gain on its investment and efforts, would enable the incubator to capitalize a seed-capital pool, and would still enable the university to receive the benefits that it set up the incubator to provide. At present, the spin-off of the RPI incubator is still just an option that has been suggested.

In the meantime, the university can make direct venture capital investments, and it has earmarked between $5 million and $9 million for such investments to be made by the university treasurer. Unfortunately for the incubator program, the fiduciary responsibility of the treasurer is such that seed financings are rarely considered appropriate investments, and to date, no incubator company has received venture capital investment by the university. Nevertheless, the incubator program is cautiously looked upon by the university as a source of venture capital endowment investments. The university has other deal flow for venture capital investments, including spin-offs from local companies (General Electric's main research and development facility, a likely source of entrepreneurial ferment, is nearby) and relationships with New York City financiers and alumni.

The Advanced Technology Development Center of the Georgia Institute of Technology

Economic conditions in Georgia, as in much of the deep South, were poor in the late 1970s. Textiles, lumber, and agriculture—all traditional Georgia industries—were depressed as a result of foreign competition, high interest rates, and the strong dollar. Because of the simultaneous depressions in some of the state's major industries, there was interest in political circles in diversifying Georgia's economy. Technology-based industries were then, as they generally are today, considered to be very desirable industries, since they are clean, well paying, and growing. Many Georgians felt that the state was an ideal location for a technology center because it has major technological universities, the center of commerce in the South in Atlanta, and an important regional airport. In addition, Georgia had the basic infrastructure necessary for high-technology industries—such as electricity, water, and good quality of life—making Georgia in general and Atlanta in particular attractive not only for indigenous start-ups but also for companies wishing to move divisions or establish new subsidiaries. This observation was emphasized by the fact that 140 Japanese firms had subsidiary companies located in Georgia.

High on Governor George Busbee's agenda for his tenure in office was the topic of economic development. From Governor Busbee and his Office of Planning and Budget came the impetus for the state government to take the lead in the effort to develop high-technology industries in Georgia. Toward this end, Governor Busbee enlisted the aid of Dr. Joseph Pettit, president of the Georgia Institute of Technology and a former dean of the College of Engineering at Stanford University, and of Dr. Thomas Steltson, vice-president for research at Georgia Tech and a former professor at Carnegie-Mellon University. These men were aware of the need for the support of a major technological university to grow a high-technology industry, especially since they had witnessed the strong roles that both Stanford and Carnegie-Mellon have played in the economic development of their respective communities and the beneficial impact of these roles. These benefits include not only the spin-off companies that a major technological university generates but also the trained graduates, expert consulting, state-of-the-art research, and modern equipment a university has to offer. Therefore, their goal, which was to develop a high-technology industry in Georgia, more accurately became how to best utilize the resources of the state to attract and found high-technology companies.

To gain insight into this problem, Governor Busbee applied for and received a grant from the Economic Development Commission of the U.S. Department of Commerce to conduct a study of the development and growth of high-technology industries. The task force that was set up to study this issue received funding from the state as well and proceeded to examine the success of the nation's other major technology centers: Silicon Valley, North Carolina's Research Triangle, and Boston's Route 128, among others. The study identified two areas in which the state could beneficially impact the establishment of high-technology industry in Georgia: aid to fledgling, homegrown entrepreneurs and assistance programs for companies interested in relocating their plants to Georgia.

However, both of the task force recommendations were already being undertaken by state agencies. The Georgia Department of Industry and Trade has general responsibility for industrial recruitment, and Georgia Tech has, for decades, performed industrial development within the state by giving assistance to small businesses. Georgia Tech has offices throughout the state that provide this assistance, and the Georgia legislature gives funding to the university expressly for this purpose. Governor Busbee and Dr. Pettit judged, however, that the Department of Industry and Trade was not properly equipped to answer the queries from high-technology industries, and although Georgia Tech's statewide system of offices was useful, it was not specifically organized to target high-technology industries; nor was it able to leverage the full potential of Georgia Tech's resources at its Atlanta campus. From this assessment, the concept for the Advanced Technology Development Center (ATDC) was developed. Located in Atlanta, on the campus of the Georgia Institute of Technology, the ATDC was first funded by the General Assembly of Georgia in 1980. The broadly defined mission of the ATDC is to stimulate the development of high technology in Georgia, with the purpose of creating new jobs.

Governor Busbee, who took responsibility for obtaining funding from the legislature for the ATDC, had a number of setbacks in his task. First, there was opposition from the board of regents of the university system of Georgia, who did not want the ATDC's funding to come out of their appropriations. This problem was solved by adding a separate, line-item approval for the ATDC in the legislature's appropriations. Second, the governor had proposed a $2.7 million funding package in which the federal government, Georgia, and private financing would share equally in the program's funding. This proposal fell through when federal funding was not available, and its failure made it very difficult to get the state funding. The problem was partially solved by the use of an abandoned high school on the edge of Georgia Tech's campus as the initial site for the incubator. One floor of the building was renovated, and the incubator was in business. Further funding from the legislature then became far easier. In Governor Busbee's opinion, it was just a matter of educating the legislature. Governor Busbee also wanted to get venture capital associated with the ATDC, but attempts to fund venture capital through the state failed.

As part of this mission of fostering technology development, the ATDC provides two services. For established high-technology companies seeking to expand operations into Georgia, the ATDC acts as an industrial recruitment agency by providing detailed information about state resources, access to facilities and personnel in the state's university system, and office space on the Georgia Tech campus. For early-stage high-technology companies, the ATDC provides a wide range of support services within its incubator unit—services designed to help entrepreneurs start, operate, and successfully build a new business. The same support staff that operates the incubator also serves as a conduit for out-of-state companies and state agencies and state-sponsored incentive programs.

The industrial recruitment portion of the ATDC is specifically targeted toward technology-related industries. Although the program's functions overlap somewhat the functions of the state's Department of Industry and Trade, the two agencies work together on projects involving the recruitment of technology firms. For the purposes of the ATDC, high-technology industries are those in which the proportion of technology-oriented workers (engineers, technicians, and other specialists) is equal to or greater than the average for all manufacturing industries (6.3 percent) and the ratio of research and development expenditures to sales is close to or above the average for all industries (3.1 percent). In its brochure, the ATDC lists the kinds of technologies it would like to recruit: aerospace vehicles and equipment, biotechnology products, telecommunications equipment, computers and peripheral devices, computer software, electronic equipment, medical devices, instrumentation and test equipment, pharmaceuticals, and robotics.

For firms that meet the qualifications of a technology-oriented industry, the ATDC will provide assistance in establishing operations in Georgia and making the best use of Georgia's state services. The ATDC offers detailed information about statewide technical resources and capabilities, research reports providing detailed information of interest to a particular firm, on-campus office and laboratory space (thought to provide a unique and desirable environment for new product development groups and research and development units of private firms), access to the sophisticated equipment on Georgia Tech's campus, and information concerning the current research in each of Georgia's major engineering universities. One very attractive feature of relocating to Georgia is that a company has to go to only one state office to receive all permits required to set up business in Georgia.

The Georgia ATDC incubator operates in a building designed for office and light manufacturing space, which was opened in 1984. A $6.1 million facility with 83,000 square feet of space, the building can house up to twenty firms in addition to the space allocated to the administration of the incubator and industrial recruitment operations. The building was funded through industrial revenue bonds and state appropriations and is located on the campus of the Georgia Institute of Technology. Georgia Tech was chosen as a location for the facility because of the industrial and technological base of the downtown Atlanta area, because of university's outstanding engineering reputation, and because of its 11,000 engineering students, who comprise a large and talented work force.

Although the initial concept for the ATDC incubator was fairly detailed, it was recognized from the start that the administration and management policies concerning entry, operations, and graduation of tenant companies would be determined after the incubator had set up operations. Entry into the ATDC is based on a fairly loose set of criteria, and the final determination of whether or not an entrepreneur is accepted into the incubator is based on a review by an admittance committee. This committee analyzes an entrepreneur's business plan using the following criteria: application and commercialization of an advanced technology, proposed products, management team, marketability of products, and ability to gain financing for the company. The admitting committee is composed of a high-technology entrepreneur, a technologist, an attorney, and an accountant or banker. All members of the committee donate their services to the ATDC for this purpose. The incubator will not accept companies that are not product-based; therefore, professionals and consultants are not eligible for entry. In addition, all companies must have a proprietary technology or product.

The incubator has a limit of 4,500 square feet per company, although not all companies use that much space. Rent is paid monthly, with the first and last months' rent paid in advance. The ATDC guarantees a tenant company incubator space for a minimum of one year but limits the length of time a company can stay in the incubator to three years. Office space in the incubator costs $9.50 per square foot per year, which is broken down into $5.50 for the space and $4 for utilities, security, housekeeping, and other services. Light manufacturing space costs $7.50 per square foot. The ATDC does not take any equity in a firm, since it is illegal for a Georgia state agency to have an equity investment in a private company. Some companies have donated stock to Georgia Tech's general fund, however.

The ATDC differs from other incubators in that it has both resident and nonresident companies as members. All member companies must undergo the same admittance process, and all ATDC members enjoy the same privileges, regardless of their location. The ATDC provides most of the shared services to incubator members at no fee, but they do not provide all the services that other incubators provide. The ATDC provides access to photocopy machines, loading docks, conference rooms, and a computerized accounting system and consulting services with the incubator's director and business staff. The incubator does not provide secretarial or receptionist services, and member companies must pay for computer time and consulting services by Georgia Tech's faculty. Each member company has access to Georgia Tech campus facilities, including laboratories, test equipment, faculty, students, and the library. Access to the Georgia Tech campus, provided by membership in the ATDC, gives each company the same status as an academic department in terms of privileges enjoyed. Following a company's admission, the ATDC provides an orientation service detailing the incubator's resources and networking capabilities. The incubator's staff then works with the new firm to develop an action plan, a document that is far more detailed than a business plan and that provides a day-to-day guide to the firm's operations. Each tenant company receives a quarterly review by the ATDC's professional staff.

Members who leave the incubator may retain their membership. Members who are not in residence at the ATDC join the program or—in the case of companies who have left the incubator—retain membership in ATDC because they receive advantages not otherwise available to them. Member companies maintain facilities apart from the ATDC because they either need more space than the incubator can provide or because they cannot afford the incubator's rents. Some companies have rented warehouse space in less desirable neighborhoods, where the rent is only $2 per square foot per year. These companies receive all the advantages of, and access to, Georgia Tech's campus, and may participate in all of the incubator's programs. In addition, the ATDC has an affiliates' program, which consists of companies not in need of the incubator's entire range of services. Affiliate companies generally have specialized needs, and these needs often require intense efforts for short periods. At times, these companies only need assistance in efforts related to obtaining funding, such as business plan preparation or referrals. There is no cost for the services the ATDC provides to the affiliate companies if the services come from ATDC's business staff. Affiliate companies must pass the admitting committee's review and must pay for access to Georgia Tech's campus or for any other services required.

The ATDC is funded by the Georgia legislature on a line-item basis, and its funding is administered through the Georgia Institute of Technology. The director of the ATDC reports to the vice-president for research at Georgia Tech, who is responsible to the university's board of regents. The ATDC has an advisory board consisting of accomplished lawyers, venture capitalists, and businessmen, and this board performs long-range planning and review functions. Its perspective is generally greater than a board of directors would normally take. From its modest beginnings in 1980, when the incubator was funded with $40,000, had only one professional and one administrative staff member, and was housed in a renovated high school building, the ATDC has grown to an annual budget of $835,000 and has ten professional and four support employees.

The incubator typically has inquiries from twenty-five to thirty entrepreneurs or companies per month and has an average of 300 inquiries per year. From this yearly deal flow, one hundred applications are received, and twenty-five companies are accepted for admission as incubator members. As of March 1986, the incubator had sixty member companies: eighteen in residence, twenty not in residence (six of them successfully graduated companies), and sixteen affiliate companies. In addition, six companies that have left the incubator have failed and are no longer operating entities. The ATDC estimates that the average turnover rate—the length of time a tenant company stays in residence—will be eighteen to twenty-four months. Once past this time frame, a company generally outgrows the incubator facility's size limitations.

The ATDC has an affiliate organization called the Advanced Technology Development Institute (ATDI), which is partly a high-technology chamber of commerce and partly a support operation for the ATDC. The ATDI is a nonprofit organization of technology-oriented businesspeople. This organization provides the admissions committee for the ATDC and a business review panel, the function of which is to review the status of a tenant company twice a year to assure that it still falls within the incubator's guidelines for occupancy. The business panel also attempts to ensure that the tenant is receiving the proper assistance from the incubator, is using the incubator's resources, and is helped with the fine-tuning of the business.

The ATDI performs separate but compatible functions in addition to the direct support it provides the ATDC. First, it sponsors a "CEO Forum"—a collection of chief executive officers, from both member and nonmember companies, who meet in a roundtable format to review a member company's operations. The members of the roundtable are intended to be peers and mentors, rather than a surrogate board of directors. Although the meetings discuss a predetermined topic, they are invaluable as a networking tool and a place to sound out potential solutions to ideas. Second, the ATDI cosponsors, with various expert organizations, three to four seminars per year on various technologies. Cosponsoring these seminars the ATDI has had seminars on such topics as surface mount technology and ergonomics. Finally, the ATDI sponsors a semiannual venture capital conference in which fifteen or more companies present their business plans to attending venture capitalists.

Helping tenant companies obtain venture capital or other postincubator funding is a primary goal of the ATDC. Although more time is needed before its success can be measured, the center has been instrumental in attracting venture capital to Georgia. There are now five venture capital firms in Atlanta, with a total capitalization of approximately $85 million. There is even one venture capital firm located in the incubator. All of these venture capital firms have been founded since 1982.

Recently, the incubator has begun to accept, as tenants, research groups from major organizations. The idea is that these firms can benefit from the incubator because they are isolated from the distractions of a major organization, are in a stimulating environment with other, noncompetitive, scientists, and have access to the students, faculty, and facilities of Georgia Tech. The ATDC refers to these groups as "landing parties," since out-of-state firms who have research groups in Georgia may be attracted to the state as they become more familiar with it. In the interim, talented researchers add to the dynamic environment at the incubator and are a potential source of spin-off companies. This concept, somewhat contrary to Governor Busbee's original concept of "growing budding scientists into embryonic entrepreneurs," and implemented at the expense of small, indigenous entrepreneurs, is a prime example of how the ATDC has deviated from its initial concept in a creative manner to fulfill its larger goals.

One common problem facing the incubator is the fact that it receives more economic development ideas and proposals than it has money to achieve. The struggle is to keep activities in a manageable spectrum that best utilizes the resources of the incubator. There are many possibilities for future expansion. One potential activity is to set up a nonprofit corporation that could accept stock from member companies and funnel the profits from this stock holding back to the ATDC.

Community Sponsored:

The Fulton-Carroll Center for Industry

To fully understand the Fulton-Carroll Center (FCC), it is important to know the background of the Industrial Council of Northwest Chicago (ICNC) and the area it represents. The council was founded in 1967 as a nonprofit organization. Its membership is made up of the owners of the industries located in an area known as Chicago's Kinzie Industrial Corridor. The corridor is a small part of Northwest Chicago where the businesses range from manufacturing and manufacturing-related industries to financial institutions and service industries. The area was a thriving manufacturing center during World War II, and many of the neighborhood's structures date back to before the turn of the century. By the 1960s, however, the area had deteriorated as industries moved to less-urbanized manufacturing centers.

The incubator is located in an area designated by the city of Chicago as a blighted slum. It is not a nice area: the Kinzie Industrial Corridor is a classic example of urban decay, and one consequence of this decay is that crime in the corridor is more than just a daily occurrence—it is a fact of life. The area was deteriorating rapidly when the council was formed in the late 1960s. The hope was to try to stem the loss of the industrial base in the inner city of Chicago. The companies that joined to form the organization were concerned both about their labor base and about their property values. A primary concern was that the corridor had already become an area where people did not feel safe to come to work. This factor led to further erosion of the industrial base, thereby increasing both the flight of manufacturing firms from the corridor and the demise of the area's overall attractiveness to industry. The Fulton-Carroll Center for Industry is only one of the council's initiatives for economic revitalization of the corridor. Despite the accomplishments of the ICNC, the corridor remains a troubled part of the city even today.

Since its inception, the ICNC has taken a variety of steps in its efforts to revitalize the area. In 1970, the corridor was included as part of an area that the Economic Development Administration (EDA) of the U.S. Department of Commerce designated as an "impact" area. The ICNC then received a number of grants from the EDA's Technical Assistance Division, along with a mandate to establish a pilot project using the model of industrial conservation as a way of retaining industry in the inner city. The council has tried to retain existing businesses and attract new businesses to the corridor by a variety of tactics. Some strategies have included programs that teach basic skills while students are performing productive tasks. For example, projects such as window weatherization of older manufacturing buildings taught rudimentary carpentry skills. Another strategy was to establish the Kinzie Industrial Security Patrol, which patrols day and night throughout the corridor for member companies. One of the strategies designed to make the area safer and more appealing to industries has been to have dilapidated vacant buildings torn down through a building code enforcement program. The council has been responsible for having forty-four buildings within the corridor demolished.

These demolition projects worked systematically throughout the Kinzie Corridor, eliminating dangerous and dilapidated facilities, until they came to the block of buildings that is now the Fulton-Carroll Center. The center comprises an entire block of buildings that the owner could not afford to have torn down, and the ICNC decided not to fund the demolition, since it felt that it would be ill-advised to have an entire block vacant. The council felt that it was important to do something more productive with the structures. June Lavelle, who has served, since the incubator's inception, as its executive director and who was working with the ICNC on building demolition at the time, came up with the idea of trying to rent the buildings out in little pieces instead of all in one big chunk. Since the council could not get any one company to come in and invest the necessary money to renovate such a deteriorating facility, it believed it might be possible to get several small companies to come in and share the risk. The result of this strategy is the incubator named the Fulton-Carroll Center, which appears to be successful in its efforts to bring in new companies, provide space for companies to grow, and generally enhance the area.

In 1973, the drive to establish what was to become an incubator in the Kinzie Industrial Corridor was initiated, and later that year, the Industrial Council of Northwest Chicago received a $1.7 million federal grant for the project. Initially, the funds were to be used for an industrial service center. This center was to provide a medical clinic, a child care center, a cafeteria, a post office, an employment office, a central alarm system with a security service, off-street parking, and a training program that would have included a licensed practical nurse program. In addition, the center would have taught health courses, clerical and secretarial courses, and English as a second language. The grant—awarded because of the council's proposal to build a pilot project in the corridor—was designed to help retain jobs and to bolster the area's slipping industrial base. It was intended to upgrade the area's labor force and its ability to meet employers' needs. The $1.7 million grant was provided by the U.S. Economic Development Administration with the stipulation that the ICNC find a 20 percent matching grant somewhere else. The ICNC members were unable to raise the $340,000 themselves and were also unable to get any banks to lend the money because of stipulations in the EDA grant that would have prevented banks from foreclosing on the building if the loan went bad. In 1974, after exhausting other avenues, the ICNC succeeded in getting the city to sell general obligation bonds to raise the needed 20 percent. But even though the bond issue was included in Mayor Daley's 1974 budget, Chicago's commissioner of planning decided that there was not really any need for an industrial service center in the corridor, and the city withheld the money. Although this eliminated the ICNC's last chance of finding matching funds, the EDA grant fortunately remained assigned to the council over the ensuing years.

It must be noted that a large portion of the success of the Fulton-Carroll Center rests on the shoulders of its dynamic and forceful executive director, June Lavelle. In 1980, on behalf of the ICNC, Lavelle succeeded in negotiations with the EDA, and the council was awarded the grant without having to meet the 20 percent matching funds requirement. She was thus able to open the Fulton-Carroll Center as a pilot project incubator. An initial goal of the project was to provide a showcase of a renovated industrial facility in addition to the incubation of companies. Because of the lack of real estate development experience among the project's administrators, the facility's renovation costs were greatly underestimated. The original plan called for $0.5 million of the $1.7 million grant to go toward repair of the physical structure, with the rest allocated for engineering studies for solar production, recycling of waste process heat, an environmental control system, and other projects. In the end, the full $1.7 million went for building acquisition and repair.

First, Lavelle bought the center's buildings for $325,000. She then began transforming these buildings into usable space. The buildings were approximately ninety-two years old and had not been maintained for many years. The windowpanes were falling out of their rotten wood; the bricks needed repointing; the elevators did not work; the loading docks collapsed during renovation; the heating system was completely inadequate and antiquated; and the roof leaked everywhere. There were a few tenants in the building, paying very substandard rents, but the facilities were in such poor condition that the rents could hardly be raised. Much of the center's initial capitalization went into simply making the space usable again; capital expenditures necessary just to keep the building functioning continue to be the largest line item in the incubator's budget. A total of $1,235,000 went for construction costs, $75,000 for engineering costs, $30,000 for an energy audit, $45,000 for accounting and legal costs, and $11,000 for the outfitting of the Business Service Center.

Occupying an entire city block, the Fulton-Carroll Center is named for two of the streets at whose intersection it resides. The center occupies three large turn-of-the-century industrial brick buildings, which are, at best, in mediocre condition. Despite the money invested in the repair and remodeling of these buildings, they still require substantial upgrading and repair, in some cases just to get the space up to building standards. The area surrounding the center is dominated by dilapidated old buildings and vacant lots littered with abandoned automobiles and refuse. The streets are strewn with smashed oil drums, car tires, parts of wrecked cars, and general trash, despite the ICNC's clean-up efforts.

Just walking around the block in this area can be dangerous. Within a half-mile radius of the incubator in a ten-month period of 1985, there were twenty-seven homicides. This rough environment poses many special problems for new company development.

Despite the drawbacks of the neighborhood, all available space within the incubator is rented. In fact, Lavelle recently agreed to rent the incubator's conference room to a small company because the conference room was not being used by the tenant companies to the extent she would have liked. Lavelle also found that they had room for an extra desk in the incubator's management offices, and they have rented that desk to a small company run by one woman. Both of these firms—the one in the conference room and the one occupying the extra desk in the reception area—are waiting for space to become available in the regular areas of the incubator.

The Fulton-Carroll Center offers its tenant companies telephone answering service, secretarial service, mailing list management, word processing, copying, and collating. The Center provides a computer, bulk mailing, Dunn and Bradstreet credit reports, a notary public, Thomas Register reference books, and a central reception area for all the tenants. The FCC also operates the Kinzie Industrial Security Patrol, which provides security. The security patrol drives the streets to minimize the number of cars that are stolen or broken into, since this can be a daily occurrence on the streets around the incubator. The security patrol seems to be one of the more critical elements of the incubator's success.

The incubator space is predominantly used for light manufacturing. The tenant spaces here are much larger individual areas than are found at places such as the Technology Enterprise Centers in Pennsylvania. The average leases are for 3,000 or 4,000 square feet and range up to 20,000 to 30,000 square feet. In fact, one company that is presently in the process of moving out, a firm named Now Furniture, has grown to occupy 75,000 square feet at the incubator facility. Now Furniture is currently the third largest foam furniture manufacturer in the country, and it is moving out because the FCC can not allot it any more space. Now Furniture was recently bought out by a Chicago venture capital firm and is moving into a newer and much larger facility. The company has decided not to move too far from the FCC, since this is the area from which it draws its employees and where it has developed its supplier networks.

Lavelle plans on breaking up the space that Now Furniture occupies, so that a larger number of smaller firms can have an opportunity for space in the incubator. It will be divided into spaces probably in the range of 2,000 to 4,000 square feet, with a couple of 20,000-square-foot areas. The FCC facility has excellent loading dock facilities, with room for about twelve tractor trailers at the dock at one time. The buildings have been redesigned so that all the tenants can easily obtain access to the loading dock for receiving and shipping materials and products.

Initially, Lavelle had no idea of what she should charge for rental space. She had no real estate experience prior to opening the incubator, and there was nothing similar to the center elsewhere whose example she could follow. There was also no place that offered office facilities with computer access, copier machines, receptionists, or telephone answering service. She arbitrarily picked a figure when she showed the first potential tenant around and quickly leased the space. Lavelle thought that if that had been so easy, perhaps she could ask a little more. So, with the next tenant, she asked for more, and then, with the next, she asked for more, until somebody balked at the price. She then came down just a little to what she thought was a competitive price for what she was offering.

Lavelle allows her tenants to sublet some of their space. This gives them the flexibility of moving into a space that is larger than they actually require and then subletting some of their area until it is needed. As the main tenant grows and eventually moves out or into a larger space, the subletter can take over the main lease for the whole space. Lavelle feels that this flexibility works to companies' advantage and ultimately to the incubator's, even though she knows that the companies generally sublet their space for more than she is charging.

The rents charged at the Fulton-Carroll Center are considerably less than those charged by privately run incubators, such as the Pennsylvania-based Technology Enterprise Centers. The $10 to $12 per square foot figure for the Paoli center is in distinct contrast to the $2.50 to $3.50 per square foot rents at the Fulton-Carroll Center. Discussions with some of the tenants at the Fulton-Carroll Center showed that the low rent was a major factor in the decision to locate there; they could afford to exist and have some office space. There was one gentleman, whose firm had been in the center since 1980, who does not believe his company would have survived without the opportunity available through the Fulton-Carroll Center. Lavelle, however, thinks that every one of these companies would have made it—would have survived on its own—without the incubator, and that all the center did was make it a little easier. It would appear, however, that the tenant was correct; many companies would not have survived and, in fact, many would not have been founded were it not for the incubator.

The center has a policy of annually raising the rent for the current companies. The longer a firm remains in the incubator, the more it pays for rent. For incoming companies, the rent remains substantially lower. This might be considered a type of exit policy. Eventually, the rent will get up to being competitive or higher than space available on the outside, thus ultimately forcing companies to look for more economical space outside the incubator. Lavelle agreed that, to some extent, this policy might entice companies to leave the incubator, but she does not consider that an exit policy. Because of this policy, however, a new firm is effectively subsidized by the older, more established firms.

Despite the initial consensus from city government, banks, and real estate developers in Chicago that this incubator idea would never work, every available square foot was rented from almost the beginning. It has been running at 100 percent occupancy since 1980. Nearly everyone who counted was convinced that no established firms would come to this area, that no one would rent the upper floors of the facility, and that Lavelle could not get company owners, let alone employees, to drive into the area. Despite the initial skepticism, the project has been a success. The land values in the corridor have risen fivefold in the five years that the incubator has been in operation. The FCC has been instrumental in turning the area into a more viable, vibrant part of the city.

It is Lavelle's hope that companies leaving the incubator will rent space across the street, or at least within the corridor. Her intent seems to be materializing, since the majority of the firms that have left the FCC have stayed within a six-block area of the incubator. This is partially because of the fact that this is the area in which the work force lives. In addition, this is where tenant companies have developed their supplier contacts. The pilot project appears to be working in its effort to revitalize the area, both by keeping industries there and by growing new ones.

People in the incubator and within this part of the Kinzie Corridor in Chicago form tightly knit groups. They stick together socially, politically, and economically. This is perhaps a significant contributing factor in the choice of new locations for graduating companies. The larger firms that make up the Industrial Council of Northwest Chicago are understandably interested in the success of both the incubator and the graduating companies. They have an economic interest in having these companies do well and stay in the area. The council members are also pleased by the fact that their real estate is now worth five times what it was five years ago. Economic development seems to have benefited everyone associated with the FCC, at least indirectly.

The Fulton-Carroll Center has a related program, also run by the ICNC, named the Chicago Industrial Finance Corporation. This finance corporation, in theory, provides eligible companies within the corridor and within the incubator with long-term, below-market loans. Projects that qualify for these loans include plant construction, acquisition, or modernization and the purchase of equipment that has a life expectancy of at least fifteen years. The finance corporation does exist, does have funds, and does make below-market loans to companies in Chicago. Its charter is not, however, limited to the Kinzie Corridor or to the incubator. In fact, it has yet to make a loan to a company in the incubator or to a company in the Kinzie Corridor. Although the Industrial Council of Northwest Chicago operates this Chicago Industrial Finance Corporation to make below-market loans as an important part of the entire Kinzie Corridor redevelopment program, the finance project seems to have had little impact on the incubator or the surrounding area.

In many ways, the development of the Fulton-Carroll Center is the story of June Lavelle and her crusade to build an incubator. Clearly, she is the driving force behind the incubator. If she had not championed the project, it is doubtful that such an accomplishment as the center could have occurred in Chicago. Lavelle takes her incubator personally. These are "her" companies; she takes care of them, and they take care of her. Lavelle has concerns about the transferability of her facility's approach to other situations, because she believes incubators and their environments are unique.

Corporate/Franchise:

Control Data Corporation Business and Technology Centers

The concept of Control Data Corporation's Business and Technology Centers (BTCs) was developed by William Norris, who was chairman and president of the company at the time. Norris, as most of the other early pioneers in the field of new business incubators, did not set out to develop an incubator as such—he was concentrating on achieving a goal. The incubator concept, as practiced by Control Data Corporation (CDC), is the means he developed by which to achieve that goal.

Norris's interest in small business began with Control Data in 1958, when it was a new small business. This interest was later piqued by his involvement with a National Aeronautics and Space Administration board that, among other things, had responsibility for funding innovation grants, which were administered through the Department of Commerce. Designed to stimulate both technical and nontechnical innovation in small businesses, the Innovation Grant program annually awarded millions of dollars to private companies and public agencies. These grants included a grant to the Industrial Council of North Chicago, which later resulted in the Fulton-Carroll Center for Industry in Chicago, and a grant to the Utah Innovation Center, which later evolved into a private incubator.

Norris observed that the United States was facing increasing competition from foreign governments and companies, which, in conjunction with advances in technology, would reduce the ability of large American corporations, such as Control Data, to continue their high employment levels. The example Norris liked to cite was that a job that took six people to accomplish in 1978 would, in 1988, require only one robot and one part-time employee. Faced with these prospects, Norris wondered where the jobs would come from and he concluded that new jobs would be created through new and small business development.

Foreseeing that small business would be a growth market, Norris conceived a mechanism by which CDC would be able to participate in this growth. He made participation in small business a corporate policy. Then he examined his available resources. CDC had sophisticated computers as well as a major investment in a computer-based training system named PLATO, and the company needed a mechanism to deliver these and non-CDC products and services to new and small businesses. To accomplish the delivery, entrepreneurs had to be attracted away from their basements and garages to a central facility with an environment supportive of entrepreneurs.

The first BTC was in St. Paul, Minnesota. The decision to locate there was determined by CDC's proximity to the area and by Norris's desire to test his ideas in an inner-city environment, where the project would contribute to the renovation of the area. With the backing of St. Paul's Mayor George Latimer, Norris targeted a warehouse district along the banks of the Mississippi called the Lowertown district. This area, which had buildings dating back to the nineteenth century, had started to deteriorate in the 1930s, so it was difficult to find a suitable building for an incubator, especially since CDC desired to have the incubator occupied solely by high-technology firms, which meant special facilities needs.

Eventually, a Lowertown facility that was suitable for the needs of an incubator came on the market. Ironically, the facility was being sold by a company whose business had been severely affected by Japanese competition, forcing the company to sell assets in order to become a more streamlined and efficient organization. The building had attributes conducive to high technology—for example, a "clean room." CDC upgraded the clean room and added an electronics laboratory, a model shop, a technical library, and computer services to the eight-story building. As the former occupants slowly moved out, the incubator built out or renovated one floor at a time. The experience at the Lowertown incubator taught CDC many lessons that subsequently shaped the policies of the rest of its incubator network.

The Lowertown incubator found that it could not attract a sufficient number of high-technology firms, regardless of the advantages the facility offered. CDC has since taken out all of the special high-technology equipment it built into Lowertown—with the exception of the clean room, which the company has been able to rent occasionally, although with some difficulty. There is no certain answer to why no more than two or three high-technology companies were attracted to the incubator. Sharon O'Flanagan, executive director of the Control Data BTC operation, feels that the reason they have not been able to attract more high-technology firms to the facility involves the business cycle of a high-technology company, which may have a narrow window, during the research phase of the firm, for the use of a high-technology facility. Moreover, research needs are highly specific, and it is difficult to offer the basic facilities that would meet the needs of all high-technology firms. After the research phase, a company may need manufacturing space rather than research facilities. A more mature company usually desires its own research facilities because of the specialized nature of the equipment it requires and because of the confidential nature of its product development.

Another finding of the Lowertown experience was that the incubator needed no entrance criteria. CDC found no advantage to trying to have one type of firm over another in the incubator. Consequently, the incubator now is open to all small businesses that are able to pay the rent. At the Lowertown facility, the annual rent is about $11 per square foot fully loaded, which gives the tenant access to all of the BTC's services. Other BTC incubator rents range as high as $18 per square foot. The incubators in the CDC network do discourage retail businesses, since there is not sufficient foot traffic to support them, and heavy manufacturing is also not generally suitable to the office environs of the incubator. There are, however, many light assembly and warehouse operations within the incubator network.

Just as the BTCs have no entrance criteria, neither do they have exit criteria. The belief is that companies will feel the need to leave on their own without any prodding. A decision to leave may be the result of the natural growth of the firm and the firm's need to manage its cash effectively. As a firm grows from start-up to a small business, it needs the services of an incubator, such as secretarial and administrative services. When it gets larger, however, the firm acquires the accoutrements of an active business, such as a full-time secretary and a marketing staff. At this point, it may not make sense for the firm to pay for the incubator's services. This situation may force the firm to leave the incubator without the incubator's staff initiating the move. O'Flanagan estimates that the point at which a firm generally leaves the incubator falls roughly betwen the twenty-sixth and thirtieth month after it enters, although there are exceptions to this generalization. Some enterprises never grow large enough to be forced to leave the incubator. The issue of whether incubators should focus on leasing space or on developing companies therefore becomes important.

BTCs offer a variety of services and products to their tenant companies. Besides the typical secretarial, receptionist, and photocopy services. BTCs offer management education services, which take a variety of forms. BTCs hold seminars and training sessions on specific topics, ranging from cash-flow accounting to marketing. In its corporate offices, CDC has developed a variety of software packages designed for fledgling businesses, and it has an employee whose job is to evaluate outside products that are appropriate for incubator companies. Some of this is PLATO software, which CDC developed for its computer-based training line of products and which has since been adapted to microcomputers so that individual businesspeople, rather than classroom-sized groups, can use the packages. Since CDC does not manufacture any microcomputers, Zenith microcomputers are used for the thirty-six–module course.

In addition to the general education packages, BTC tenants have access to at least two consulting sources. The first, called either the Management Assistance Office or the Cooperation Office, depending on the location, is set up by the community in which the BTC is located. This office is designed to help the entrepreneur before the business is incorporated. The second source of consulting comes from the BTC's Business Development Services Office, within the incubator itself. This office is set up to help the businessperson survive the trials of entrepreneurship. A third potential source of consulting is from the seed-capital fund. Assistance from the fund is contingent, of course, upon receipt of outside funding as well and generally takes the form of assistance that any venture capital firm would offer.

The BTCs, sometimes through CDC or sometimes on their own, also offer other services, such as travel discounts, telemarketing services, human resource counseling (offered to all CDC employees to help workers deal with stress, personal problems, and so forth), centralized purchasing (which provides discounts for purchases of anything from furniture to fleet automobiles), and insurance.

One unique service the BTCs offer their tenants is electronic networking on a data base, the BTC Electronic Network, that is tied into a national data base named The Source. This service was established after CDC discovered that its network of tenants could be a resource for individual tenant firms. Using this electronic network, tenant companies can advertise, handle barter deals, set up distributor relationships, and whatever else comes to mind. With more than 700 companies in its incubators, this electronic network can be a valuable resource. The Source data base has more than 60,000 subscribers, giving BTC tenant companies significant visibility.

One of CDC's incubator goals is to make it as easy as possible for an entrepreneur to start his own business. One tactic the BTCs employ to achieve this goal is to accommodate entrepreneurs who require small spaces or short lease terms. Another tactic is the use of what they refer to as the "outpatient basis" entrepreneur, whereby an entrepreneur can rent twenty-four hours of space per month in the incubator. The entrepreneur has the right to use this time whenever he wishes during the month at a fee of about $150 per month. Typically, the entrepreneur is employed elsewhere and uses this time to develop a business plan for the prospective company. CDC feels that this gives the entrepreneur the opportunity to test the entrepreneurial world without giving up his job. Even after a company has left the incubator, a BTC tries to ease the entrepreneur's burden by making its services available, albeit for a fee. One BTC has even initiated an alumni-networking program. Non-BTC-resident companies are also welcome to use BTC services on a pay-as-you-go basis, although BTCs usually do not have a formal associates program.

Typically, a BTC will have a staff of four or six and a building maintenance crew. The staff will include the incubator manager, a receptionist, a word-processing clerk, a business analyst, and, at times, other support staff. A BTC manager must perform a variety of functions. First, he or she must be a real estate manager and rental agent. The incubator cannot afford to have empty space for very long, since most incubators are not heavily capitalized. The incubator manager must be a counselor as well, although a business analyst lends support in this function. In addition, the BTC will have an advisory panel consisting of businesspeople from the community—lawyers, accountants, bankers, and others who donate their time both as a method of public service and in enlightened self-interest. Because its time is limited, the advisory panel typically concentrates on firms with the most promise of success. This process helps to naturally eliminate tenant companies with the least chance of business success.

From the beginning, CDC intended to replicate its incubator concept in other communities, since Norris's goal was to help small businesses become job creators within the community and preferably within inner cities. Although CDC did not initially target community governments and economic development agencies as a market to penetrate, this marketing strategy emerged as a CDC focus. This occurred because the communities and CDC had common objectives and needs—communities desired to create jobs, and the incubator concept appeared a viable job-creation tactic; and CDC had expertise to sell, needed a local partner, and was also committed to creating jobs. The process of setting up an incubator with the assistance of a community organization involves three stages: setup of the incubator, establishment of a seed fund, and management assistance in running the incubator.

The process of setting up an incubator is more than just pulling together a building, an administrator, and an advertisement for entrepreneurs. To set up an incubator, CDC charges a one-time license fee of $50,000. In return, CDC brings its technical experience to the establishment of an incubator: site selection, construction, renovation consultation, coordination of architects with construction firms, hiring and training of an incubator manager, recruiting of an advisory panel, building of community support, and a three-year public relations program. CDC also gives the BTC access to its electronic network and to the software products it has developed for the incubator companies. For a fee of $15,000, BTC managers take part in annual week-long training sessions, which give them the opportunity to network and exchange notes and provide CDC with insights on ways to improve the program.

The second step in the establishment of a CDC incubator is an optional seed-capital and management-assistance fund for the community. For this service, CDC charges a negotiable fee of between $50,000 and $100,000. The company then sends a three- or four-person staff to the city for up to twelve weeks. This team determines the best type of fund for the community, then writes the business plan for the fund's operations. The business plan will include information on target investments, growth of assets, investment guidelines, deal flow, and operating guidelines. CDC itself, although in the incubator business for profit, does not invest in these funds or in the companies directly. Its profits come only from the services it provides, and the services seem to be priced at or near cost.

A representative of the general partner of the seed pool will perform the evaluation of prospective investments. This representative comes from within the community and has certain restrictions on allowable investments. The community seed-fund and management-assistance program is not limited to the incubator, since its first priority must be to return a profit to investors; nor is the fund limited to investment within a specific geographic area, although a certain portion of a fund's pool is likely to be set aside for local investment. CDC feels that the existence of a seed-capital fund with indirect ties to the incubator is a necessary ingredient for small business development within a community. The seed-capital fund is also expected to develop a network of relationships with national venture-capital funds to give exposure to larger funding sources for its seed-investment portfolio companies. Half of the communities in which BTCs operate have seed-capital funds, but most of the earliest BTC communities do not, possibly because the importance of the seed fund was not initially understood by the communities. The use of seed capital is an investment strategy many people do not understand, making seed capital difficult to attract. O'Flanagan feels that the ideal size of the seed-capital fund is $4 million, although this figure varies with the size of the incubator.

The third and final component of the CDC incubator concept is the ongoing relationship of the BTC with CDC and with the other BTCs in CDC's network. CDC has structured its relationship with associated BTCs in three ways. The first structure is the CDC-owned incubator, in which CDC owns the incubator building and operates the incubator. Within this structure, CDC receives all revenues from the incubator's operations, which for the most part consist of rental income but also include the purchase of products. CDC also pays all incubator expenses and, therefore, receives any losses. The second structure is the joint venture, in which CDC will participate in the building's financing. This participation will often take the form of loan guarantees or of a commitment to cover a deficiency of the incubator's operations. The third structure is the license agreement, by which CDC agrees to provide its family of products and services, but the licensee owns and operates the incubator. As of this writing, CDC has seven company-owned incubators, nine joint-venture incubators, and six licensed incubators.

As noted, CDC is in the incubator management business as a for-profit operation. Although the fees for CDC's services may seem high, they should be considered in comparison with other processes. The fee of $100,000 to $150,000 to have CDC set up an incubator may not be exorbitant compared to the cost, for example, of preparing a prospectus for a company soon to go public, which typically costs in excess of $250,000, or for the establishment of a restaurant, which now costs about $200,000.

CDC has more than fifty people in its corporate offices dedicated to the incubator management business. Half of these are involved in the development of products and services for the incubators. The other half are involved in operations such as real estate and site selection, franchising, accounting, and the day-to-day tasks of incubator start-up. A fully loaded fifty-person operation can be expensive. CDC receives income from the real estate of its seven company-owned facilities and fees from all its incubators. Thus far, space in the incubators that are over one year old has been approximately 83 percent leased, which is above the traditional 75 percent cash-flow break-even level. However, because many of the CDC facilities are in inner-city neighborhoods, it is doubtful that they can charge sufficiently high rents to make this rule of thumb valid. Nor do the incubators purchase significant quantities of equipment from CDC—CDC receives a yearly fee of $15,000 from the twenty-five current BTCs, which contributes a total annual revenue of $375,000. The cash-flow operation of CDC's incubator management business is not known, since CDC cost and profit figures are not available.

It was CDC's stated goal, when the incubator management business was initiated, to have 100 BTCs in its network by 1990. This goal has since been modified to 100 BTCs by 1995.

O'Flanagan would like to see CDC operate a venture-capital fund to take advantage of the deal flow to which CDC has access, but she anticipates that CDC's first priority will be smaller units in communities of perhaps 12,000 to 40,000 persons. Communities of this size may be the most difficult in which to operate a successful incubator. Although the average CDC incubator size is over 90,000 square feet, CDC has BTCs that range from under 5,000 square feet to 329,000 square feet (this largest incubator is the Lowertown BTC, which, in addition to the eight-story building, has since acquired a warehouse of 107,000 square feet). O'Flanagan feels that the optimum incubator size is between 50,000 square feet and 75,000 square feet, since this is large enough to support a professional staff yet not so large as to become unwieldy.

CDC's incubator management program has been criticized in some circles. According to O'Flanagan, this criticism is the result of a well-meaning program named City Venture Corporation, which Norris initiated. In 1978, Norris gathered together a group of chief executive officers of large, Midwest-headquartered corporations. At this meeting, Norris proposed that each of the CEOs, armed with the resources of their corporations, would apply their talents to the redevelopment of inner cities, with the primary objective of creating jobs for minorities. CDC's contribution would be the application of their then embryonic BTC concept. Although the goals of this group were admirable, the execution of the concept was insufficient to make it a self-supporting enterprise. CDC lost money on several incubators because site selection for these BTCs, which CDC did not control, was more on the basis of job creation than on real estate principles. The less-than-favorable performance of these City Venture Corporation incubators has since negatively affected the reputation of Control Data's incubator management program.

With more than two million square feet of office space within the incubator network, housing 738 companies, the CDC incubator venture can certainly claim one measure of success. The company also notes a 93 percent success rate among tenant companies, meaning that these companies are alive, not merged, bankrupt, or otherwise out of business. At the Lowertown facility, which has the longest track record—over six years—the success ratio is 84 percent. In addition, these companies now employ an aggregate of 7,800 persons, 6,100 of whom have jobs that have been created since tenant companies moved into the incubator network. Control Data's BTCs have graduated a total of 353 companies.

Technology Centers International

Technology Centers International, Inc., (TCI), an incubator management company founded in 1976, operates seven Technology Enterprise Centers (TECs) nationwide. With principal offices in Montgomeryville, Pennsylvania, the TCI incubators are run for profit, with certain parallels to a franchise operation. There are seven TECs now operating in the United States, and another five or six are in the planning stages. TCI is the brainchild of Loren Schultz, who started the company after successfully founding his first incubator facility in Montgomeryville in 1976.

Schultz is an entrepreneur who has started several successful companies—most notably, Decision Data Corporation of Horsham, Pennsylvania, now a company with $100 million in revenues. It was through some of his early experiences with an employer who encouraged totally separate work groups within the same company that Schutlz developed his concept for TCI incubators. Since TCI's founding, he has devoted his time, energy, capital, and experience to aiding small business ventures and promoting their growth. The original center, although comparatively small, has seen the birth and growth of more than fifty companies and claims a 90 percent success rate for start-up firms. This experience in Pennsylvania led Schultz to carry the concept to other sites with facilities of varying sizes.

TCI incubators provide a facility with a central entrance, a reception area, conference rooms, and modular, cost-effective space. Services include secretarial assistance, such as word processing, copying, and telephone answering. Also provided is a computer system with a limited capacity to network. Schultz believes that one of an incubator's primary strengths is the creation of a highly synergistic environment within them. This synergy can be generated by the atmosphere of similar struggles and successes among the tenants. Entrepreneurial business managers who work in close proximity to other entrepreneurs have an opportunity to share and learn from one another. It has been suggested that this synergy can best be achieved by filling an incubator with firms of a similar type (for instance, an incubator full of software companies or light manufacturing firms). The TEC concept, however, holds that synergy can best be created by bringing together under one roof a wide diversity of entrepreneurial talents. This concept is reflected in the fact that TEC incubators are operated with no entrance criteria for new firms. All a prospective tenant is required to do for admittance is to pay the first and last months' rent in advance.

Besides having no entrance criteria, the TCI incubators have no exit policy for tenant firms. So long as a company can continue to pay the rent, it can stay. Schultz has structured the incubator in this fashion because he believes that an exit policy is not needed. He believes that successful companies want to be perceived as independent, without the "stigma" of being in an incubator. Consequently, he does not like the word *incubator*, because it carries many negative associations in his opinion. It connotes that firms are being nurtured or watched after, and Schultz does not believe entrepreneurs like that. This is one of the reasons TECs are called Technology Enterprise Centers, not "Technology Incubators." Important to the image issue is that TECs be perceived as providers of space and assistance to professionals, not as coddlers of firms unable to make it on their own.

Schultz prefers that no retail or distribution companies locate within his centers, but TCI does not have an fixed exclusion policy. In fact, several of the Lansdale, Pennsylvania, incubator's companies are retail operations. The rents at TCI's incubators, which range between $10 and $12 per square foot, are competitive with the local market or slightly below market level. There is not, however, any pretense of trying to provide low-cost space.

The combination of multiple services and reasonable rent implies that the incubator leasing business is not a high profit margin venture. Another, and more profit-oriented, intention of the TEC incubators is to provide a screening mechanism for possible venture capital kinds of investments. As part of the TEC concept, Schultz has set up a venture capital funding network for companies within the incubator. As it is designed, there is a Local Fund associated with each incubator, which is capitalized from local investors. Each Local Fund also makes an investment in a master fund called the Technology Fund—a national fund with larger capitalization and an orientation toward larger, later-stage investments.

Although specific figures on the size of the master Technology Fund are not available, Schultz does say that TCI has been working to increase its investment potential. The fund is set up as a partnership, is managed by a professional staff, and is capitalized by both local funds and non-TCI-affiliated limited partners. The purpose of this fund is to generate high returns for its investors through investments made around the country in firms that the Technology Fund's directors deem worthy. The Technology Fund can invest in any firm that its directors choose, without regard to whether or not the firm is associated with a TCI incubator. The TCI incubators do, however, offer a window on a variety of potential fast-growth firms. The Technology

Fund comprises half of the financial system that Schultz has designed for the TECs. The other half is what he refers to as the Local Funds.

Under the TCI incubator concept, the Local Fund is a $3 million to $5 million pool that has been raised in the area in which the incubator is located. Information on the sizes of individual Local Fund pools is not available; size may vary from incubator to incubator. Although the Local Fund is also not specifically mandated to fund only companies within its incubator, the incubator does act as a point of concentration for deal flow. Through the incubator, investors have the opportunity to examine a variety of companies in one location, track their progress, and consider investments in any of them. The Local Fund, like the Technology Fund, can be used to invest in any firm that the directors choose. Its purpose is to provide seed-capital financing for local companies that may or may not be in the incubator.

The difference between the Local Funds and the Technology Fund is primarily a matter of scale. The Local Fund is supposed to provide more start-up seed capital, whereas the Technology Fund is designed to provide later-stage financing. Generally, the Local Fund makes the first investment in a firm; the size of that investment could range from $50,000 to $400,000. As a general principle, the Local Fund plans to stage its investment in two phases, since small businesses always seem to need more funding than was originally envisioned. The Local Fund will not invest more than 10 percent of its total capitalization in any one company. If an investment by a Local Fund continues to look good but the firm still needs more money in order to grow, the Technology Fund is meant to provide this second-stage financing, with investments ranging from $200,000 to $750,000.

Schultz feels that TCI's incubator network has been an effective mechanism to filter and funnel companies to possible investment funds. Through this system, he can gain access to a large number of small start-up companies, and through this network he feels he can efficiently keep close tabs on them. Consequently, with ten incubators in operation and approximately fifty companies in each, there would be a network of 500 companies from which to consider investments from the Technology Fund.

The criteria for receiving investment dollars from these funds is far different from the criteria for getting into the incubator. Getting into the incubator takes only a company's first and last month's rent in advance. Receiving an investment from either the Technology Fund or the Local Fund requires proof of significant profit potential. Generally, the funds use the same criteria as a venture capital firm. However, unlike the typical venture capital firm, the funds do not seek a major or controlling piece of a company's equity. Schultz suggests that they are looking for only a 15 percent to 35 percent equity position. He believes that if over 50 percent equity is required for the success of the investment, it is not a good investment. This position stems from the belief that taking a large piece of the company also detracts from the entrepreneur's motivation. It is also interesting that, as another invest-ment filter, Schultz first looks not at the company's management, as do most venture capitalists, but at the company's market niche. His opinion is that the market cannot be changed, but the new company's team can be modified.

Each Technology Enterprise Center has a center Champion. The Cham-pions are under contract to both the local investment fund and the Technol-ogy Fund. Their contracts with the TECs require them to find and identify technology-oriented companies with, says Schultz, "tremendous growth po-tential." Each Champion then presents these investment opportunities to the funds' management. The Champion should be a person with considerable management experience in both small businesses and large organizations who has the ability to evaluate an idea and offer advice on its viability. The Cham-pion is available to the tenant firms to help with business planning, market research, policy development, cash-flow analysis, and goal setting. Once an investment has been made by one of the funds, the Champion becomes re-sponsible for monitoring the investment. Within this function, the Champion must assure that the funding is being used in an effective way to meet speci-fied objectives and must periodically report the company's status to the fund management. Regardless of this connection with the funds, ITC literature says that the center Champion's "real obligation is to the entrepreneur" that he or she must help them get the best possible deal, and is therefore their Champion.

The Champion, therefore, has a dual role: to assist the young business and its representative in the search for financing and to be on contract to the Local and Technology funds. Ideally, this individual is to champion the cause of the small company to the Local and Technology funds, which, in turn, will call upon other center Champions, TCI staff, and outside business advisers to evaluate the recommended business for possible investment. Once one of the two funds has invested in a company that has been recommended by the Champion, the Champion often receives a share of ownership in the new firm. The Champion is working for the funds and is on contract to them but, is also championing the cause of the incubated company. Therefore, the Champion plays a mixed role—assisting in the monitoring of the investment, thereby theoretically assuring that the funding is being used in an effective way to meet the objectives of the Local or Technology Fund, and, at the same time, attempting to act as the small company's representatives to these finan-cial groups. The center Champion does not work directly for the firms in the incubator, does not necessarily have an office in the incubator, and is not restricted to seeking investment opportunities from within the incubator.

In addition to the opportunity for profit through investment in selected companies, incubators can provide income through their real estate. In sev-eral of TCI's incubators, real estate appreciation can be extremely profitable. When unused or underutilized property has been refurbished, the incubator facility, as well as the surrounding real estate, can increase in value. The increased commerce that the incubator stimulates is itself a value-added function and shows that the incubator can have a strong, positive impact on the host community.

The incubator facility in Montgomeryville, Pennsylvania—the first TEC and the location of TCI headquarters—is in an attractive rural setting. The site is approximately twenty-five miles to the north of Philadelphia center in a town with a population of under 1,000. There are a large number of industrial park developments in this area of Pennsylvania, and the Montgomeryville Center is located on the fringe of one of these parks. Most of the companies in the nearby industrial park appear to be, if not high-technology, at least "clean" industry. This facility is an older, single-story commercial structure, dating from perhaps the 1950s or 1960s. It is not a "flashy" looking building on either the inside or the outside. Schultz has chosen to allow no individual company names on the exterior of the TCI incubators—only a single sign identifying the building as a Technology Enterprise Center adorns the exterior.

The Lansdale Center is a converted turn-of-the-century glue factory in Lansdale, Pennsylvania, a town of approximately 16,000. In Paoli, another small Philadelphia suburb of about 6,000 people, TCI has taken over and remodeled an unused grade school.

The companies in Schultz's incubators span a wide range of types. Since there are no entry criteria, there is no central conceptual focus pulling together the companies in the incubators. This is a conscious decision, since TIC believes this diversity provides an important cross-cultural experience. In the three TECs mentioned here, tenants ranged from a patent attorney office to a resin-glue processing firm.

The Lansdale TEC has an auto repair shop that repairs car and truck engines and a small computer-consulting firm, as well as a company that sells office equipment. There is a small business for importing and selling turret lathes to industrial clients and another that is a personnel management consulting firm. At the Montgomeryville incubator, there is a company that manufactures little pocket flashlights on which a company's logo can be printed for promotional purposes. There is another firm that manufactures credit card access machines for office copiers.

Multiple additions over the years have left the Lansdale facility a varied collection of buildings. There is a 1950s addition with some office space toward the front, an old glue dryer out back in one of the larger shed buildings, and in a separate building, an auto repair shop, off to one side. At the Lansdale facility, originally a glue factory, very little has been done to enhance appearances. From the street, it appears to be an older building landscaped with grass; from the back, it is a dilapidated warehouse. An old, but still usable, railroad spur comes in along one side; the roof leaks; the wooden floors are cracked, worn, and crooked; and some of the outbuildings are rickety. Several tenants have been able to negotiate rent breaks for doing needed structural repairs to their part of the facility. There is not, at this facility, the perception of success that may be imperative for attracting certain types of entrepreneurs and their fledgling firms.

In Paoli, the facility is a converted schoolhouse, the main part of which dates from the 1920s. There is also a large addition, probably from the 1960s. In contrast to its policy in the Montgomeryville and Lansdale centers, TIC has invested heavily in remodeling the Paoli facility. The site is located in an attractive, older residential neighborhood less than a block and a half from a train line to Philadelphia. The incubator not only is able to take advantage of the former school's parking facilities but also rents part of its excess parking space to the train station for the Philadelphia commuters. The Paoli TEC director is negotiating with the stationmaster to have the railroad take care of security on the parking lot and snow removal in exchange for parking privileges.

The large playground that was associated with the school has been turned into a public park, and the park land has been deeded back to the city, which now maintains it. This provides a serene and picturesque setting for the facility. In an energy conservation effort, TIC has reduced the size of the windows in almost all of the rooms and has added extra insulation to many areas. Separate heat pump and air-conditioning–heating systems were added so that the individual companies could pay their own utilities. Since there is still a main heating system in the buildings, this TEC will heat the building to a very minimal level; any further heating will be handled by the individual companies with their own heating units.

The Paoli center provides a variety of spaces. Most of the large classroom spaces in the school have been divided up. The space available starts at about 150 square feet for a small office. The offices of this size are rented out with a desk and chairs, so that a small company can easily move into a furnished office with the central receptionist of the incubator answering all phone calls and fielding all visitors. There are a few of these small offices, a number that are about 300 square feet, and several that are 400 square feet. The facility also offers a few spaces that are 600 square feet and two or three at about 1,200 square feet. The large school auditorium can be used, at least initially, by any of the companies for presentations or training films. To make the auditorium income-producing, an effort is being made to find a small theater or film company that could take full advantage of the space. The Paoli center also has a gymnasium in which several health clubs have expressed an interest.

The larger classrooms at the Paoli center have been divided up with concrete block walls that are sheetrocked and painted over, and new carpeting has been added throughout. There is an attractive U-shaped drive to the front, left from the school setup, which gives the building a dignified facade. The remodeling has been tastefully done and should attract companies for which appearance is important. Rents at this center run from about $10 to $12 per square foot, plus utilities.

The Montgomeryville incubator and headquarters building, although newer than the Lansdale facility, offers similar spaces. The remodeling that has taken place over the years has left the structure with a varied layout of hallways and office spaces. The loading dock at Montgomeryville is one room off the main hallway, with a garage door outside. It does not have a raised ramp for large truck deliveries or shipping. The Lansdale facility, in contrast, has a full loading dock with capacity for five tractor trailers. Half of the dock is available to all tenants and half is leased to a national freight trucking company. The trucking company also leases a small amount of warehouse space at the Lansdale incubator and uses its portion of the loading dock as a local pick-up point. The converted school in Paoli has never had a loading dock.

Although TCI has developed a 20,000-square-foot facility in Montgomeryville and a 150,000-square-foot facility in Minneapolis, Schultz is of the opinion that the ideal incubator size ranges from 40,000 to 60,000 square feet. The size of all the Technology Enterprise Centers is in distinct contrast to the Industrial Council of Northwest Chicago's Fulton-Carroll Center for Industry, which has 340,000 square feet.

Schultz says that the TECs are set up to create companies, not jobs. He feels it is important to keep what he considers a correct priority: companies create jobs as a byproduct when the intent is to create a successful company. On the other hand, he feels that successful companies are rarely created by programs or companies that are set up to create jobs.

Private:

The Rubicon Group

The Rubicon Group, Incorporated, is a high-technology incubator located in Austin, Texas. Founded in 1983, Rubicon is privately funded and operates as a for-profit corporation. Partly as a result of its private funding sources and partly because of its high-technology focus, the Rubicon incubator concept is more closely akin to the venture-capital process than perhaps any other incubator in the country. It was founded on the premise that the reward system for seed capital and for entrepreneurs could make a for-profit incubator a viable concept. Most other incubators attempt to leverage the talents of would-be entrepreneurs by providing consulting and other shared services. They make their profits through the rents paid by tenant companies. Rubicon, however, sets up joint ventures with its client companies, providing most of the overhead services required by an emerging firm in return for a significant portion of that firm's equity. Rubicon's profits come only through its ownership position in its client companies. Because it does not own a building, it does not receive rental income and does not refer to the companies with which it has joint ventures as "tenant" companies.

Rubicon was cofounded by Stephen A. Szygenda, an accomplished entrepreneur and former professor at The University of Texas at Austin, and by J. Jette Campbell, a former partner at a big-eight accounting firm and a partner with a major Austin real estate development company. In 1981, Szygenda sold his company, Comprehensive Computing Systems and Services, to COMSAT and began looking for other ventures to pursue. During his career as an academic, entrepreneur, and consultant in technology, Szygenda saw many technically brilliant individuals who were woefully deficient in the business world. Campbell, through his experience in working with emerging companies, had recognized how many new businesses fail because of poor management practice. These observations led them to conceive the notion of a business designed to develop the sophisticated technologist and would-be entrepreneur into a successful businessperson. Together, Szygenda and Campbell developed the initial concept into a detailed operations plan and proceeded to raise funds for the project. Armed with a ten-page business plan, and "enough background planning to fill a 300-page volume," Szygenda and Campbell approached a carefully selected group of local investors. One evening at Szygenda's house, they outlined their concept to potential investors. They presented it, not as an incubator—since they were not familiar with the new business incubator concept that was just beginning to emerge around the country—but rather as a new venture partnership. From that presentation they raised the initial $2 million capitalization for Rubicon.

Szygenda and Campbell initially expected that the limited partners would form the network from which the partnership's deal flow would come. To Rubicon's founders, the criterion of networking was as important in selecting potential limited partners as the financial capacity to participate in the partnership's funding. As it turned out, the deal flow came from many sources, and the firm was flooded by more than 300 business plans within the first year. Rubicon was further surprised to find that nearly all of the firms that were eventually brought into the organization had a product already being marketed.

Rubicon was developed with the idea that no money for company operations would have to come from the individual entrepreneur. Just as a venture-capital company would make funds available for a firm to hire a staff to perform the functions necessary for an emerging company, Rubicon would provide a staff to perform those functions for each of its client companies. In addition, Rubicon, like any traditional venture-capital company, would pay for these services only until the firm had sufficient cash flow from its operations to afford to support them itself. Rubicon generally structures its joint venture so that it agrees to support a company through two years of operations, with the company's cash flow contributing whatever it can in the interim. In theory, therefore, funding for a firm's operations comes either from Rubicon or from the company's cash flow. In reality, the expenses of a growing operation are great enough that all available funds from operations go into expanding the business, and Rubicon's contribution to the company ends up being fairly constant throughout the first two years. Therefore, Rubicon pays for everything, from the company's rent to its marketing costs to its staffing costs, during the two-year period.

Most of the tasks of running a company are performed by Rubicon's staff, which has been as large as twenty-five individuals in five departments (with some overlap of people among departments) but which currently numbers nineteen persons. This staff performs far more services than an incubator typically provides. In addition to the receptionist, word-processing, and janitorial services usually available in an incubator, Rubicon seeks to provide comprehensive services in five areas: finance and administration, legal, technical, marketing and sales, and business education. In the finance area, Rubicon provides all accounting, financial planning, bookkeeping, and financial education. Rubicon's staff helps computerize the company's record keeping and teaches the company's president how to perform such tasks as cash-flow management, financial projections, and payroll management. The administration department oversees company policies and procedures as well as personnel and facilities issues. The legal services provided by Rubicon consists of an in-house counsel. Technical services provided include those of an engineering staff, technical writers, computer specialists, and provision of data base and technical software packages. When necessary, a client company will have access to professional consultants in addition to the technical advice offered by Rubicon's advisory committee. Rubicon's marketing and sales service consist of everything involved before the actual introduction of a product. Following product introduction, the client is supposed to develop a sales force and distribution network, so that the company will be able to subsist independent of the incubator after graduation.

The final service area provided by Rubicon is in business education. Each entrepreneur with whom Rubicon has joint ventures receives 160 hours of entrepreneurial education over the course of the two-year program. "If anything," says Szygenda, who served as Rubicon's president and chief executive officer for the partnership's first two years, "this is not enough education." The goal of these classes is not to teach the client companies everything they need to know about running a business, but rather to sensitize them to the types of problems they will encounter in the business world. The very broad range of topics covered in the classes, which Rubicon says gives their entrepreneurs a "street-smart" MBA, includes corporate structure, wills and trusts, planning, scheduling, the mechanics of business insurance, legal structures, management, finance, and other topics. Rubicon intends that this education will enable the entrepreneurs to exist and to weigh decisions independent of the incubator when the two-year period is over.

Rubicon does not require that a prospective company submit a business plan to be backed by the venture partnership and the incubator. It was the feeling of Rubicon's organizers that the people whom they were seeking to help either would not have a business plan or, in many cases, would not be capable of producing a realistic one. If these entrepreneurs were sophisticated enough to produce a reliable business plan, they likely would not be proper candidates for Rubicon's services and would have other capital sources available to them. However, each client company is required to write a business plan, with the aid of Rubicon's staff, within the first 120 days of residence in the incubator.

Rubicon's entrance criteria have many similarities with venture-capital investment criteria. However, Rubicon's concept of how to grow a company, and the resulting differences in deal evaluation criteria, differentiate it from a traditional venture-capital pool. Instead of a business plan, which all venture capitalists require for screening purposes, Rubicon looks primarily for people with superior technical qualifications and ideas. Whereas a venture capitalist will first require that the core of a superior management team be in place before it invests, Rubicon intends either to bring in new management or to develop current management into a team capable of growing an emerging company. It is less necessary that a Rubicon client have experience than that he have technological expertise and common sense.

Rubicon's other entrance filters are similar in nature to venture-capital investment criteria, except that the investment size and potential sales figures are scaled down. Rubicon looks for a technology with some proprietary feature. The market for the product should be large enough to support the entrance of a new company into the market and should have a high growth rate so that the company does not have to take significant amounts of market share away from other companies. Although the venture-capital firm wants an investee company's products to have an identifiable market of $100 million or more, Rubicon can be content with a company whose market is well under $50 million. For both venture capitalists and Rubicon, a company's market should be growing by a minimum of 15 to 25 percent, and a 50 percent growth rate is both desirable and not particularly rare. These market size and growth figures are a reflection of the goals venture capitalists and Rubicon have for their respective companies. Venture capitalists want their companies to achieve a minimum sales level of $40 million to $60 million within five years. Without these initial market-size and growth figures, this goal would not be achievable. Rubicon, however, considers a company highly successful if it can achieve sales of $15 million within five years; it can therefore be content with smaller market sizes.

Part of the difference between venture-capital partnerships and Rubicon, although each is structured as a venture partnership, stems from basic differences in their philosophies and goals. Venture capital is organized to achieve capital gains. Any income that is not capital gains does not maximize the partnership's return to the limited partner because of the penalizing tax rate on ordinary income as opposed to capital gains income. This indicates that a venture-capital firm must be able to hold its investment instruments, without a holding penalty, until it can distribute the instruments' proceeds subject to capital gains tax. Legally, the venture-capital partnership either must be self-liquidating or must be organized for a predetermined period, or else the partnership can be classified as a corporation and will lose its tax advantages. These advantages include no corporate tax; the ability to distribute investment securities without a limited partner becoming immediately liable for tax on unrealized gains (the tax liability begins when the limited partner sells the security and has a realized gain, at which time the partnership's historic cost of the security becomes the basis for the security's valuation); and the compounding of returns without taxes until liquidation. Venture-capital partnerships are, therefore, organized for a seven- to ten-year period, a timeframe that enables an orderly investment, growth, and liquidation cycle.

Rubicon, in contrast, wants cash flows from its ownership position in previous client companies to support the development of later rounds of incubated companies. It has a mixed strategy for realizing both cash flows and capital gains income from its investment portfolio. The value Rubicon intends to create for its limited partners is not capital gains so much as a growing organization whose stock has value because of a diversified growth portfolio, whose working capital and investment capital needs are satisfied through the cash flow generated by its ownership position in previously incubated companies, and which can provide a yield on its stock through the payment of dividends from the proceeds of capital gains and surplus cash.

Rubicon was originally organized as a limited partnership. Following the initial funding of $2 million in 1983, Rubicon raised $1.5 million in a second financing round in early 1985 and another $787,000 in late 1985. In January 1986, Rubicon incorporated and began to seek another round of financing. One stated reason for its change in organizational status is that the advantages of being a partnership have already been exploited to their maximum extent. A second reason for the change is that in seeking the additional funding a corporate organization will enable it to cast a wider net for investors. A third reason for corporate structure is that it will enable Rubicon to attract a corporate or institutional partner. Rubicon would like to have such a partner to give it broader backing, deeper pockets, and access to technology opportunities. A partner of Rubicon's choosing would likely be a broadly based, technology-driven company with strong interests in electronics and computers.

One of the most difficult tasks in building an incubator is finding the proper staff to manage the facility and companies. For Rubicon, management is considered the single most important ingredient in the success of an incubator, because Rubicon's approach is to bring in technologically oriented businesspeople who need significant assistance and advice to become successful entrepreneurs. In this context, the incubator's management has as much to do with the success of a client company as does the entrepreneur or his idea. Yet finding management with the proper experience to work in an incubator is a difficult task. There is no education available that teaches how to simultaneously manage a variety of different companies, each with distinct technologies, different stages of maturities, and varying degrees of business expertise. Running an incubator is different from managing a corporation with several divisions, since each division is managed with the goals, objectives, and financial constraints common to the rest of the company. An incubator is more akin to a conglomerate, since a conglomerate consists of many diverse companies. But conglomerates work because they are decentralized, whereas an incubator such as Rubicon centralizes functional activities. Szygenda feels, therefore, that even an experienced entrepreneur must make some significant adjustments in organizational and managerial orientation to become the president of an incubator.

Evidence of how much emphasis Rubicon places on management is the fact that its key officers and advisors are given equity in the Rubicon portfolio as an incentive to maximize the client companies' value. Originally, each of five Rubicon officers and the Advisory Board shared automatically in the equity of client companies, although this has changed since the company restructured itself from a partnership to a corporation.

To understand what percentage the officers and advisers originally received, it is necessary to examine the structure of a typical Rubicon joint venture. Rubicon generally took at least 50 percent of a company's equity. Of Rubicon's equity, twenty-five points (25 percent, or 12.5 percent of the total company) went to the management of Rubicon as the general partner's carried interest. Of these twenty-five points, each of the five key officers received two points, for a total of ten points. Other key employees shared in a pool of stock as a sort of profit-sharing plan. The general partner's carried interest, as much as fifteen points, was split among the founders. In addition to these twenty-five points, which came out of the limited partners' share and went to the general partner, one and one-half points were awarded to each of the ten members of the Advisory Board. Therefore, of the total equity purchased by the Rubicon partnership, 40 percent went to management or advisers of Rubicon. This represented 20 percent of the total equity of a company, since Rubicon received half of a company's equity in return for its investments. With the change from a partnership status to a corporation, all carried interest rights in Rubicon had to be converted to shares in the corporation. As a consequence of this change, not all officers currently have an ownership position in the company. Although the compensation package has not yet been finalized, Rubicon does intend to continue its policy of granting an ownership interest in the portfolio to key officers.

Members of Rubicon's Advisory Board are highly respected individuals within Austin's business and academic community. The level of expertise on this board is interesting. On the technical side, Rubicon has a former chairman of the computer science department, the former head of a major engineering department, and an associate professor of electrical engineering, all at The University of Texas at Austin. One Advisory Board member is a member of the National Academy of Sciences and another is a member of the National Academy of Engineering. In the nonscience areas, board members include a partner at a major Austin law firm, Jette Campbell, and other businessmen and entrepreneurs. As noted previously, members of the Advisory Board were initially given 1.5 percent of Rubicon's interest in each company Rubicon backed. The board was set up with this remuneration because Szygenda felt that with so much equity, each board member would have the incentive to make a significant investment of time in building client companies. This profit-sharing schedule was changed so that Advisory Board members now receive equity only in the companies for which they directly consult.

One innovation that Rubicon has installed in its compensation package is to give each of Rubicon's officers, including the president, the same rather modest salary. This reflects two purposes. First, because a large portion of their compensation is in the form of stock, the officers have a significant and common incentive to maximize the value of Rubicon's portfolio. Second, this eliminates politicking among the officers, since there is no opportunity to gain additional salary at the expense of other officers. Rubicon also provides a minimal salary to the founders of each of its client companies. Rubicon feels that the officers of client companies, by not having a high salary, keep their focus fixed on the building of a company and, by extension, their own fortunes.

Client companies have generated a very heavy work load for the management of Rubicon, despite its large staff and high-powered Advisory Board. This was the determining factor in Rubicon's decision to drop an associates program whereby Rubicon staff would have worked with companies with which Rubicon did not have a joint venture. There was a point in Rubicon's start-up phase at which the founders thought it practicable to make each of the five departments a separate profit-and-loss center by allowing outside consulting. There were entrepreneurs who were willing to give Rubicon 5 to 10 percent of their company just to have access to Rubicon's consulting staff. The associates idea was abandoned after the work load with resident client companies became too large. Another reason there is no associates program at Rubicon is that management felt that it was an activity that would dilute the efforts of the primary goal: to help build new companies and to share actively in the risks and rewards that the venture might bring. For this reason, Rubicon does not make relatively passive venture-capital investments, nor does it own a building.

Instead, Rubicon planned to invest in twelve to fifteen companies and to concentrate resources on developing them. When it became apparent that ten companies would sufficiently tax Rubicon's resources, it stopped taking applications from potential client companies. The founders of Rubicon projected that 50 percent of the client companies would fail within two years. So far, three companies have discontinued operations. Rubicon recently discontinued joint ventures with two other companies after determining that they did not have sufficient upside potential to warrant further investment. These firms are still ongoing concerns that function independent of the services of Rubicon. Although they were disappointed, the entrepreneurs of these companies seem to have left Rubicon on good terms. Four of the remaining five companies are projected to have in excess of $500,000 in sales in 1986. None of these companies is projected to have more than $15 million in revenues within a five-year period, although each has the potential of having $7 million to $10 million of profitable sales within this period.

As it was planned, all of the client companies were high-technology companies. Six of the original companies were software companies, with products including microcomputer software for financial institutions, fund-accounting software for nonprofit institutions, insurance and employee benefits analysis software, structural design software, and personal productivity software for microcomputers. Other companies are hardware- or systems-related. From this process, Rubicon management has learned to be more patient in selecting client companies to take advantage of the quality of deals available.

Rubicon is small compared to many other incubators. It has only 15,000 square feet of space to rent client companies. It is anticipated that client companies either will not move far from the incubator's location or will stay in the space where they already are and assume the rent payments. Because the incubator-backed companies will eventually occupy a large amount of space, Rubicon's management does agree that the real estate profit option is a viable profit-making operation. For Rubicon, even the client companies that are past their two-year limit but are still in the immediate vicinity will benefit the company indirectly through the fostering of a culture of high-technology entrepreneurship. There was some thought in early 1985 of trying to open similar venture-partnership incubators in Houston, Dallas, and San Antonio. After some deliberation, it was determined to postpone this plan until the original incubator had proved successful.

Rubicon is less than three years old and probably has at least another three years to go before it is mature. Maturity, in Rubicon's case, means that it has achieved cash-flow break-even and that income from its investment in previous client companies is providing all of its cash requirements. If it takes five years from the beginning of the initial investment cycle to the point at which this cash-flow break-even occurs, then Rubicon is growing its companies about as fast as a successful venture-capital operation would. Although companies are capable, in many cases, of throwing off cash at earlier stages in their development, they are likely to need this cash for operations in order to actualize their full growth potential. This differs from other incubators, whose cash flow is provided from rent and whose high initial costs for facilities are capitalized over the life of a mortgage.

Just as there is a growth cycle for emerging companies, there is also one for incubators. The process of incubating companies takes time, as Rubicon is discovering. Rubicon is now seeking another stage of financing to facilitate the transition to a new management and operational structure. In October 1985, Szygenda stepped down as president to pursue other entrepreneurial ventures, and George Pearson, a businessman with twenty-five years' experience in large organizations, became president. Pearson's focus is on developing the operational aspects of Rubicon and its client companies. Under Pearson's leadership, Rubicon has reevaluated the performance potential of its client companies, with the result that five of its ten portfolio companies either were spun out of the incubator or had their operations discontinued. Rubicon has developed a revised set of selection criteria that focuses strongly on technological feasibility of the product and its market opportunity and focuses less on the technological expertise of the entrepreneur. Rubicon has also expanded its networking opportunities to try to improve deal flow and its evaluation and advisory capabilities. Finally, Pearson has developed a more focused approach to operational policies and procedures, an effort that has streamlined Rubicon's operating system.

8

The Future of New Business Incubators

The new business incubator can be an effective and innovative approach to helping entrepreneurs in their start-up phase with reduced overhead costs, expert assistance, and financial backing. Because there is such a great need to leverage resources in a hypercompetitive environment, the concept will become a more important mechanism for developing entrepreneurial talent and for contributing to economic development.

The Incubator Potential

Incubators have been established by a variety of organizations, including universities, private entrepreneurs, public or private partnerships, nonprofit associations, and management organizations on a franchised basis. They are diverse in their structure and operations. In most locales, there can be considerable value in the reduced overhead costs, access to specialized services and equipment that entrepreneurs could not otherwise afford, skilled and experienced business advice and assistance, and a supportive environment that arises from a number of colocated new businesses. New business can thus operate with a minimum of rented floor space and can have access to shared services—secretarial, shipping and receiving, fabrication shops, storage, and special technical equipment. Incubators can produce small business firms, dynamic growth firms, and a more stable and balanced infrastructure for entrepreneurial activity. They can also strengthen ties for further commercialization to research and industrial parks and the venture capital industry (see figure 8-1).

For the entrepreneur, a new business incubator can hold a variety of benefits. In addition to the operational benefits that come with being associated with an incubator facility, entrepreneurs gain access to, as well as education and training from, critical business know-how. This is especially important in such areas as management and marketing. They may also be able to tap important technical support in such areas as engineering, computer sciences,

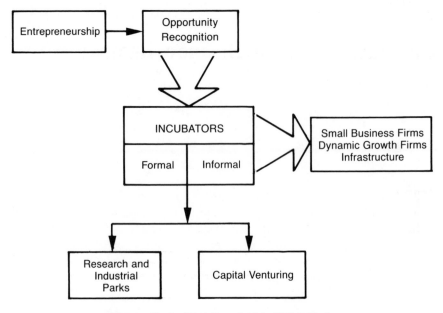

Figure 8–1. The Incubator Potential

biotechnology, medicine, and other technology-related disciplines appropriate to their businesses. Furthermore, they may gain access to important professional support, particularly in the areas of finance, accounting, and law. Finally, they may gain access to a network of other entrepreneurs and business connections and may therefore reap both the tangible and intangible benefits that a network affords.

But the incubator idea is still new and experimental. Consequently, some incubators will fail; others will be modified; and still newer variations on the concept are likely to emerge. Experience will be the most important teacher in this process.

Those who are planning incubators must realize that the incubator is not a panacea for economic woes. It should be only one tool or mechanism in a broader economic development strategy. It can contribute to economic diversification, but the process takes time. Results do not appear overnight. Consequently, it is important to have realistic expectations and to understand the work involved in developing a viable incubator.

Incubator managers and directors must continually seek ways to implement critical success factors in incubator operations. The more that these factors are incorporated in the incubator, the greater the chance of success for tenant companies. Building companies requires not only resources but also an understanding of the entrepreneurial process. By integrating the two, those who run incubators will have more effective operations.

Entrepreneurs must be mindful of their own interests and must fully understand the incubation process. Being in an incubator requires no less work and dedication than not being in one. Each entrepreneur must ultimately be responsible for his or her own company. Consequently, the entrepreneur must ask questions and evaluate options. He must be aware of what he gives up and what he gets through an association with an incubator, especially one that takes equity in the firm as part of the arrangement. The match can be effective if the "chemistry" is right and if each side knows what is involved in the association.

New business incubators will continue to increase in number in the United States and in many other countries. They will provide more alternatives for economic development, more opportunities for diversification, and more choices for entrepreneurs.

Caveats to the Incubator Movement

As the number of incubators increases some important concerns must be kept in mind. The National Business Incubation Association listed 143 incubators as of April 1986, and forecasts 1,000 by 1990. As a result of this growth, some forecasters have indicated that new business incubators will be the most prominent form of economic development in the United States in the 1990s. Is all of this enthusiasm justified? The answer is "maybe." It will take time to determine whether incubators are a truly revolutionary concept in economic development, an evolutionary development that fills a specialized niche, or a passing fad. Obviously new business incubators are perceived by many persons as the answer to a variety of problems. But new business incubators are not going to solve all problems related to economic development, job creation and successful business growth. This book has reviewed some of the stimuli for the establishment of incubator units. But if the role of an incubator is not properly perceived, and if the incubator is not effectively organized, then it will probably fail. In such instances, the incubator will fail not because the concept itself is flawed, but because the concept was not properly matched to the requirements of the organizers.

Many firms require five years or more to achieve a level of maturity and viability in the marketplace. This is especially true for technology-oriented firms. Other firms—such as travel agencies and insurance companies that operate in some incubator units—are not the most appropriate firms on which to base a long-term evaluation of an incubator, since in many cases these firms would probably have started without the help of an incubator.

Consequently, incubators will take time to mature and show impact. Due to the development cycle associated with start-up ventures, it may be at least five years before an incubator produces an ongoing stream of successful companies. To judge the success of an incubator any earlier may be premature. This has serious implications for the supporting entities of incubators, whether they be private investors, corporations, universities, or government entities. A commitment to the incubator concept must take this developmental cycle into account, or both the incubator and the tenant companies may not have the benefit of time.

Many firms will fail despite the best efforts of incubators. An incubator cannot completely overcome poor management or undercapitalization, the two most common reasons that a business fails. The incubator can help the entrepreneur in both of these areas, but the incubator cannot operate the business in lieu of an entrepreneur. Since many incubator managements have no selection criteria for the companies that occupy space in their incubators, there is no barrier to entry for entrepreneurs who may lack the sense of urgency and other motivations to build a successful business. So, some business failures should be considered an accepted hazard of the incubator process.

Effective incubator management is critical. Without effective management of the incubator and proper support for the tenant companies, the incubator will fail. There are three important components in running the incubator: conceptualization and organization, facilities management, and consultation with tenant firms. Each element is essential. Yet few individuals have the experience to do all three well at the same time. Thus the ability to network becomes all the more necessary. The consultation aspect, for example, can be a formidable task since it is difficult for one person to provide advice to a dozen companies with diverse technologies, management problems, marketing constraints, funding constraints, different stages of development, and various levels of talent.

In the conceptualization and organization phase, fund raising plays an important role and should probably be completed prior to the initiation of operations, since incubator management must concentrate on the task of incubating companies.

The incubator is a method to achieve a goal, whether that goal is jobs, profit, or technology development. The ultimate incubator goal, however, should be to develop companies that eventually will be viable outside the incubator. The incubator is thus part of the developmental phase in a company's growth and maturation cycle. All incubators have a for-profit objective in the sense that the companies which they help develop must be profitable to survive on their own.

While we have learned a great deal about the incubator concept, there are still important issues that must be addressed. Some of these issues are:

Do incubators lower the rate of failure of new business start-ups? If so, to what degree?

To what degree are or can universities be a source for entrepreneurs and firms, especially in regard to new technical firm start-ups?

To what degree are incubators influencing or encouraging people to start new firms?

How critical is a Champion to the success of an incubator?

How does the cost of company development within an incubator compare to the cost outside an incubator?

To what degree do incubators contribute to job creation and economic development over time?

What is the return on investment for incubator investors?

What are the most appropriate evaluation techniques and criteria for entrance into an incubator?

What are the impacts of exit criteria for tenants over time?

What is the effectiveness of industry specialization within an incubator?

Through further research, especially through longitudinal studies, we will develop insight on these and other issues related to the incubator concept.

Trends in Economic Development

As shown in figure 8–2, seven major trends are affecting the direction of economic development:

1. Technology as a resource
2. Hypercompetition in domestic and international markets
3. The role of invention
4. Government as stimulator
5. Entre/intrapreneurial development
6. Innovative capital formation
7. Collaborative relationships

Technology is more than a thing, a gadget, or even a process. It is a self-

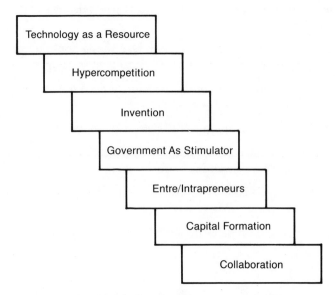

Figure 8–2. Trends in Economic Development

generating resource that is not consumed in the process of use. Consequently, it is an important form of economic wealth.

Hypercompetition is forcing a reassessment of our individual and collective responses to the marketplace. Fierce domestic and international competition for scientific, technological, and economic preeminence is forcing communities and regions to leverage all their resources—human, technological, and financial—to compete effectively for vibrant and diversified economies.

The United States is experiencing an unprecedented burst of invention. Myriad technological advances are occurring with incredible speed and frequency. The ability to commercialize these innovations will have direct and immediate economic consequences.

Federal, state, and local governments are trying to find positive, yet noninterventionist, approaches to encouraging entrepreneurship and technological diversification. They seek to create jobs, provide benefits to the small business sector, and push technology. The creation of an environment that promotes entrepreneurial activity has become a more important focus in government policy development.

People with raw energy and a proclivity for risk taking are the drivers behind economic development. These entre- and intrapreneurs are breaking tradition and are providing a dynamic source of creative and innovative enterprises.

Innovative capital formation is the catalyst for the entrepreneurial process. Mechanisms for providing seed capital as well as an expanding venture capital industry are helping to build new ventures.

Finally, creative collaborative relationships are being formed between business, government, and academia. These ties are forging new opportunities for the commercialization of ideas and are accelerating the technology transfer process.

Within the context of these major trends in economic development, new business incubators can play a unique role. They can help provide a business and education infrastructure that is conducive to entrepreneurial activity. They can provide a practical mechanism for risk taking and risk sharing in the early and most uncertain stages of business development. They can promote cross-institutional collaboration. They can help to create jobs by increasing the chances of success for emerging companies. Consequently, the new business incubator will be a more widely used mechanism for linking talent, technology, capital, and know-how.

Appendix

Setting Up a New Business Incubator

Excerpted from *Small Business Incubators: New Directions in Economic Development—A Handbook for Community Leaders* (Washington, D.C.: U.S. Small Business Administration, Office of Private Sector Initiatives, March 1985).

Framework for Market Research

Step One: Establishing a Working Group

The involvement of key individuals and organizations in the community is critical to the success of an incubator, both in its formulation and implementation. No organization from outside a community can develop a successful incubator without the community's interest, demand and support. Because of their visibility, incubators quickly become the focal points for economic development and small business assistance.

Three levels of organizational involvement are present in the development of an incubator facility:

1. Lead sponsor organization—the initiator,
2. Local working group—responsible for plans through implementation,
3. Other community organizations—provide support and publicity.

Lead Sponsor Organization

To complete a feasibility study or other activities related to development of an incubator, someone must initiate the project and assume leadership.

The primary duties of the initiating individual or organization consist of:

- Identifying and contacting key individuals to serve on the working group,
- Convening preliminary meetings of the working group,
- Overseeing collection of information for the feasibility study, and
- Contacting other local organizations not represented in the working group to get information for the feasibility study.

The initiator will usually come from one of the following organizations:

- Local government,
- For-profit corporation,
- Local development organization (i.e., Chamber of Commerce, 503 Company), or
- University or Community/Junior College.

Local Working Group

The local working group is responsible for formulating a sound plan and sticking with it through its implementation. The working group should consist of approximately six to eight key members of the community. The members should be decision-makers in their respective organizations who can commit resources. In addition, the group should be representative of a broad range of community organizations and skills.

The primary responsibilities of the working group include:

- Completing the necessary market research,
- Gaining support for the incubator from other community organizations, and
- Providing guidance and/or direct involvement in critical phases of the project's implementation.

Worksheet One provides a list of potential members for a local working group.

Potential working group members should be contacted early in the process. The first contact(s) should be with individuals who are likely to participate in the working group and who would be influential in encouraging others to get involved.

A list of individuals or organizations expressing an interest in the project should be compiled so the interested parties can be recontacted later. Some members of this group may be in a position to commit financial resources to the project. If commitments cannot be secured from several key members of the community, the lead sponsoring organization should reconsider proceeding with the project.

Worksheet Two provides a format for making contacts with prospective members of the working group.

Other Community Organizations

In addition to the sponsoring organization and local working group, other organizations should be contacted to determine interest and support for an incubator. While these organizations only will be involved peripherally, their participation will strengthen the network of support available to the incubator project.

Possible contacts include:

• Influential business persons (from small or large businesses),
• Key members of local government, and
• Representatives from organizations listed in the small business support network, e.g., SCORE, SBA, University/Community Colleges, Inventor's Council, etc.

Step Two: Analysis of Local Economic Base

To determine if a community has a market for incubator space, three major aspects of the local economy should be analyzed:

1. Characteristics of large corporations in the area,
2. Level of entrepreneurial activity in the community, and
3. Supply of, and demand for, incubator-type space and support services, by industry type.

Characteristics of Large Corporations

Analyzing the characteristics of local large businesses is important because it provides information about potential markets for new small businesses. Many communities have conducted an analysis of their large companies' major suppliers. Often the findings indicated that, to a large extent, local big businesses import a significant amount of supplies, raw materials, and support services from outside the local economy. With such information, some communities have convinced their large companies to "Buy Locally", creating large and stable markets for new businesses.

In addition to providing a potential market for local small businesses, major businesses are often the community's primary source of spin-off firms. The type of industry and level of spin-off activity should be considered when deciding on the type of incubator to establish (e.g., high technology, manufacturing, services, etc.)

Worksheet Three provides a framework for analyzing the characteristics of local large corporations.

Worksheet Four is a format for gathering information on suppliers to local major companies.

Assessing Level of Entrepreneurial Activity

It is also important to assess the level of local entrepreneurial activity in a community. The rate of new business start-ups, number of business permits issued, patents issued, number of home-based businesses, etc., are indicators of potential demand for incubator type space and support. These indicators also help to identify the growing sectors of the economy—information which a sponsoring organization might use to decide what type of incubator businesses should be recruited.

Worksheet Five can be used to gather data on the level of entrepreneurial activity.

Supply and Demand for Commercial Space

The third aspect of the local economy to be examined is the real estate market. For an incubator to succeed, it must fill a real market need. Therefore, the supply and demand for below-market space must be carefully assessed. To determine the supply, an inventory of available commercial space should be taken.

To be effective, the space supply inventory should be broken down by types of commercial property (i.e., retail, manufacturing, office space) as well as by prevailing market rates. If the inventory shows the community has a glut of cheap manufacturing space, then obviously, the incubator sponsor needs to look very critically at any proposal to establish an incubator for manufacturing firms.

An additional element included in the analysis is the type of lease arrangements available. Often start-up businesses cannot commit themselves to long-term leases.

The demand side of the equation is equally as important. A review of approximately fifteen incubator feasibility studies suggests that surveys and interviews of realtors, existing new small businesses, banks, local development companies, etc., can give a general indication of the level of demand in the community for incubator-type space. To repeat, it is important to break demand down into specific types of commercial activities.

Worksheet Six provides several matrices to aid in the assessment of the supply and demand for commercial space.

Step Three: Assessing the Small Business Support Network

It is important to examine the degree to which a community has formalized its support for small business. If a survey of the community reveals there are few formal business development programs/services offered, this fact should be considered when deciding whether to establish an incubator.

Small Business Support Network includes:

- Availability of pre- and continuing business workshops and courses, sponsored by local SCORE chapters, community or junior colleges or chambers of commerce.

- Active organizations supporting small business issues with a strong membership from the small business community.

- Availability of financing for start-up and expansion of small businesses including favorable lending policies by lending institutions, establishment of venture capital, 503, SBIC companies, etc.

- Favorable city/county/state business climate including taxation policies, ease of acquiring necessary licenses and permits, zoning restrictions, etc.

- Formal and informal, public-private programs providing specialized technical assistance, such as invention evaluation services, import/export counseling, etc.

- Community awareness of importance of, and contributions by, small business including whether local media provides information about small business issues or of interest to small business owners.

Incubators complement and draw upon other local small business support programs.

A Network is particularly important to the potential success of incubator tenants.

An incubator itself will have limited local resources at its disposal and operational costs will be affected if a community lacks a strong small business support network and sponsors should help develop or strenghten a local network before they begin incubator development.

If surveys and interviews show a strong support network does exist, the information can be used to: 1) identify potential resources and support services for incubator tenants, and 2) identify other local groups with similar objectives that may be valuable additions to the incubator development working group.

Worksheet Seven is a sample survey to assess the strength of the small business support network.

Step Four: Analyze Data, Define Goals, and Establish Objectives

Analyze Data

When Steps One through Three are complete, the sponsoring organization should have a good indication of the following:

- Level of interest and support of the working group for an incubator facility,
- Supply and demand for commercial real estate by business type,
- Current and potential level of entrepreneurship in community, and
- Strength of small business network in community.

The next step is to analyze each category of information in terms of:

- Major strengths and/or weaknesses,
- Gaps in information collected and/or resources identified, and
- Strategies for gathering additional information, gaining other resources, involving other key organizations.

Define Economic Development Goals and Objectives

A community's economic development goals and objectives provide the driving force for the design of an incubator facility. However, prior to setting specific objectives and/or deciding on the type of incubator facility to establish, the working group must reach consensus on the community's broad economic development goals.

Example:

Community economic development goals for _____

1. Promote Economic Growth

2. Diversify Local Economy
3. Revitalize Deteriorated Commercial Area

Once the overall goal is established, the working group can develop specific, measurable objectives.

Worksheet Eight is a checklist to help communities formulate broad economic development goals and specific objectives.

Establish Appropriate Focus for Incubator

After the goals and objectives are established, the working group must insure the incubator is developed within their framework. The specific objectives determine the focus, type and structure of the business incubator.

Example:

Goal	Objective	Incubator Focus
Promote Economic Growth	*Create specific number of jobs*	*Recruit labor intensive firms, e.g., manufacturing*
or	*Create new businesses*	*Recruit prospective or out-of-area businesses, e.g., to supply local large corporation*
Diversify Local Economy	*Develop hi-tech sector*	*Recruit hi-tech firms, establish strong connection with area universities*
Revitalize Business Area	*Rehabilitate commercial building*	*Recruit any businesses which will locate in project*

Worksheet Nine includes a list of issues to be addressed in establishing objectives for an incubator.

Steps for Successful Implementation

Step One: Collect Information on Other Incubator Projects

The information gathered in Steps One through Four will help organize a targeted search of information on existing incubator facilities. The key to this research effort is to limit the research to those facilities in similar size cities with similar objectives.

Without spending too much time or money, getting information on different successful incubator projects will help contribute to the success of a new facility by helping the sponsoring organization avoid the common problems experienced by others.

Worksheet Ten lists the type of information available on each facility and lists the sources for such information.

Printed Information on Incubator Facilities

Small Business Incubator Resource Summary. U. S. Small Business Administration, Office of Private Sector Initiatives, 1441 L Street, N. W., Suite 720A, Washington, DC 20416. List of written material about small business incubators.

Incubator Times. U. S. Small Business Administration, Office of Private Sector Initiatives, 1441 L Street, N. W., Suite 720A, Washington, DC 20416. Newsletter.

Incubators for Small Business. U. S. Small Business Administration, Office of Private Sector Initiatives, 1441 L Street, N. W., Suite 720A, Washington, DC 20416. Lists contacts for 31 incubators, 7 pp.

Small Business Incubator Sample Information Package. U. S. Small Business Administration, Office of Private Sector Initiatives, 1441 L Street, N. W., Suite 720A, Washington, DC 20416. News clips and project summaries, 23 pp.

Small Business Incubators: A How To Guide. Community Information Exchange, National Urban Coalition. National Urban Coalition, 1120 G. Street, N. W., 9th Floor, Washington, DC 20005, (202) 628-2981. [for sale.]

Starting a Small Business Incubator: A Handbook for Sponsors and Developers. Illinois Department of Commerce and Community Affairs and the U. S. Small Business Administration, Region V. Reviews incubator characteristics, steps in developing incubators and sources of financial and technical assistance. Includes profiles of 10 incubators, August 1984, 79 pp. [for sale.]

The Industrial Incubator. Purcell, Mia. Information Service Report No. 27. National Council for Urban Economic Development, 1730 K Street, N. W., Washington, D. C. 20006, (202) 223-4735. Describes and compares seven incubator facilities, highlights critical decisions made in designing, financing and managing a successful incubator, February 1984, 20 pp. [for sale.]

Business Incubator Profiles. Temali, Mihailo, and Campbell, Candace. Minneapolis. Hubert H. Humphrey Institute of Public Affairs, University of Minnesota, 909 Social Sciences, 267 19th Avenue South, Minneapolis, MN 55455, (612) 376-9996. A survey of 50 business incubators for the Institute's Cooperative Community Development Program, 1984, 130 pp. [for sale.]

Contact Incubator Managers

After reviewing available publications, it is valuable to speak with one or more managers of incubator facilities to get their first-hand comments and suggestions. A number of incubator managers provide background information on their facility upon request, some of it for a small fee.

Visit at Least One Incubator Facility

No matter to whom you speak or what you read, you will not understand what incubators are until you actually visit a facility. While on-site, it is definitely worthwhile (if possible) to visit with some of the tenants. They are often the best spokespeople for the incubator concept.

Contact a For-Profit Incubator Development/ Consulting Firms

If a community decides to explore the feasibility of developing an incubator, but lacks the in-house expertise or time to devote to the project, it should consider contracting. There are a number of private corporations which provide assistance with the development of small business incubators.

Step Two: Identify and Select a Suitable Site and Facility

An incubator site will have to meet the specific needs of the type of business to be located in the facility, (e.g., manufacturing, retail services, R&D, etc.) because each type of commercial activity has different space and location requirements. When the sponsor decides the type of commercial space it requires, there are three possible sources of existing buildings: private, public or corporate owned properties.

The site supply information collected during the inventory of commercial space should list the available privately owned facilities.

In addition, a survey should be made of various local public organizations to locate any publicly owned, vacant commercial land and/or buildings. Local city and county governments, school boards or federal agencies such as U.S. Small Business Administration and U.S. Department of Justice should be included in the survey. A public entity acquires commercial property through the exercise of eminent domain, through foreclosures or, as in the case of a school board, the property may be publicly owned but no longer occupied. If a suitable facility is publicly owned, a sponsor may be able to negotiate a favorable sale, lease or transfer of ownership.

Private corporations should be surveyed to determine their plant use or expansion plans. Several incubator sponsors received buildings as a donation from a local corporation. Generally these buildings were ones which the corporation planned to vacate in the near future.

A major constraint on site location is the financial resources available. The majority of incubator facilities were developed using existing buildings by financing acquisition and renovation with public funds. There are, however, several examples of incubator projects in newly constructed facilities. Obviously, new construction requires a substantial financial commitment— one which most economic development organizations are not in a position to make.

Other factors to be considered in the site selection process include:

• Access to major transportation routes
• Shipping and receiving areas, if required
• Adequate storage
• Adequate space for conference rooms and other "shared" space requirements
• Potential for expansion
• Local zoning laws

- Compatibility with surrounding area
- Proximity to supplies (depending on type of tenants)
- Parking (for tenants, customers, clients, etc.)
- Rental space in general area for incubator graduates
- Condition of building structure
- Estimated renovation costs
- Annual utility expenses
- Security

Worksheet Eleven provides a framework for listing and evaluating potential sites.

Step Three: Arrange Financing

One of the most critical steps in the implementation process is finding the financial resources to make the project happen. Once the decision is made to proceed, sponsors can begin to identify the financial needs and potential sources of funding for the project.

The next Section of the *Handbook* is devoted to the financing aspects of incubator development. A model of typical financial requirements is included, as is a survey of both public and private sources of funding. Finally, case studies which detail the financing sources used to finance twelve successful incubator projects are presented.

Step Four: Develop Management for Facility

One of the critical steps to a successful implementation strategy is development of a management plan. At this stage, the following decisions are made:

- Organizational structure, and
- Operational policies and procedures.

The organizational structure outlines who will determine basic policies and who will implement them. A decision making group may be a formal Board of Directors selected from the original working group and provided for in by-laws of an new organization or corporation. Some incubators developed by existing organizations are governed by officers or the board of the parent group.

Advisory councils serve some incubators by recommending policy changes, assisting with publicity and public information and monitoring community response.

Generally, an incubator manager is responsible for implementing policy and operational procedures.

Operational policies and procedures will include decisions about tenant screening and graduation policies, types of services offered to tenants, type of and responsibility for publicity and operating budget and financing.

Information from the survey of other incubator projects (Worksheet Ten) will be a valuable aid in determining policies during this step. Worksheets at the end of the Financing Section will help develop a budget and financing mechanisms.

Worksheet Twelve includes outlines for developing a Management Plan.

Step Five: Develop a Marketing Strategy

The data gathered in the market research phase should provide the basis for the marketing strategy. This information is essential to determine a pricing strategy for rental space and shared services, the location of the incubator facility, and the products and services needed by the major suppliers in the community and the tenant firms.

When the market research is complete, a promotional strategy should be developed to recruit potential tenants and identify markets for products and services of and for the tenant firms. The strength of the local working group will greatly increase the success of the following promotional strategies:

- Development of stronger relationships with other organizations.
- Targeted mailing to small businesses, business groups, major local corporations.
- Press releases announcing acceptance of tenant firms, opening of incubator, agreements with participating organizations.
- Incubator brochure detailing benefits of facility.
- Development of incubator newsletter and/or provide information about incubator to other organizations' newsletter.

- Cosponsor seminars of interest to prospective tenants. Subjects might include Venture Capital, Starting Your Own Business, and Computers for Small Business.
- Sponsor opening ceremony with participation of key community, business, political leaders.
- Meetings with business leaders to inform them about the incubator facility.

Market Research and Project Implementation Worksheets

Worksheet One: Incubator Working Group

Organization: Name:

Local Government   (select 1)

_____   Mayor

_____   City Council Member

_____   City Manager

_____   Economic Development Director

_____   Other (specify)

Private Industry   (select 2: 1 from large business,
                                              1 from small business)

_____   Chief Executive Officer

_____   Vice President, Purchasing

_____   Vice President, Public Affairs

_____   Real Estate Developer

_____   Architect

_____   Law Firm

_____   Accounting or Management Consulting Firm

_____   Engineering Firm

_____   Construction Company

_____   Other (specify) _____

Private Lending Organization   (select 1)

_____   Commercial Bank

_____   Savings and Loan

_____   Venture Capital Group

_____   Other (specify) _____

Local Development Organization   (select 1)

_____   Chamber of Commerce

_____   Local Development Corporation

_____   Industrial Development Council

_____   Private Industry Council

_____   Other (specify) _____

Community Organization   (select 1)

_____   Kiwanis Club

_____   Jaycees

_____   Other _____

_____   Other _____

Educational Institution   (select 1)

(a) University

_____   President

_____   Professor of Business or Planning

_____   Director, Small Business Development Center

_____   Other (specify) _____

(b) Community or Junior College

_____   President

_____   Professor of Business or Planning

_____   Director, Small Business Development Center

_____   Other (specify) _____

Worksheet Two: Community Power Structure Matrix

Organization (Address, Telephone Number)	Key Contact (Name, Title)	Contact (From, Referral, and Reason)	Contact Made (Date, Method)	Notes (Avail. Resources, Express Interest, Follow-up Needed)

Worksheet Three: Analyzing the Local Economy—Characteristics of Local Large Corporations

List major corporations in the community. Note business type, gross sales, number of employees. Indicate with yes/no: 1) if company is part of local economic development network, 2) if company has a formal small business sub-contracting program, and 3) if company spawns a high number of spin-off businesses.

COMMUNITY CORPORATE PROFILE: _____ *(name of city/town)*						
Company Name	Type of Bus.	Gross Sales	No. of Employees	Part of Ec. Dev. Network	SB Sub-Cont. Program	Has high no. of spin-offs

COMMUNITY CORPORATE PROFILE: _____
                                    (name of city/town)

Company Name	Type of Bus.	Gross Sales	No. of Employees	Part of Ec. Dev. Network	SB Sub-Cont. Program	Has high no. of spin-offs

Worksheet Four: Analyzing the Local Economy—Company Supplier Analysis

List company's major suppliers, supplier's location, product/service provided, annual dollar volume and if supplier is located outside of community.

Example:

Company Name: *ABC Company, Smithtown, CO*

Supplier Name	Business Location	Outside Comm.	Prod./Serv. Provided	Annual Dollar Volume
a. XYZ Co.	Jeansboro, NE	X	sheet metal	$200,000
b. Barb's Big & Acctng	New York, NY	X	accounting serv.	$ 75,000
c. Mary's Janitorial Inc.	Dallas, TX	X	janitorial serv.	$ 25,000
d. Supplies Co.	Smithtown, CO	X	nuts & bolts	$ 60,000

Tabulation of Results

When the analysis of the major corporations is completed, the information can be tabulated in the format provided below. The information will provide a good indication of potential markets for new businesses in a community.

Example: Total dollar volume of purchases from "outside" suppliers by type of product/service purchased by major company.

Company Name	Raw Material	Prof. Services	Other sup. Services	Manuf. Goods	Office supplies
ABC Co.	20,000	70,000	50,000	1,000,000	60,000
MNO Co.	10,000	100,000	25,000	500,000	10,000
TOTAL	30,000	170,000	75,000	1,500,000	70,000

Company Supplier Analysis

Company Name: _____

Supplier Name	Business Location	Outside Comm.	Prod/Serv. Provided	Annual Dollar Volume

Company Name: _____

Supplier Name	Business Location	Outside Comm.	Prod/Serv. Provided	Annual Dollar Volume

Total dollar volume of purchases from "outside" suppliers by type of product/service purchased by major company.

Company Name	Raw Material	Prof. Services	Other sup. Services	Manuf. Goods	Office supplies

Worksheet Five: Analyzing the Local Economy— Assessment of Entrepreneurial Activity

The following worksheet can be used in gathering data on the level of entrepreneurial activity in a community. Results should be viewed as an indicator of potential demand for below-market space and new business support services.

Data:	*Sources:*
Number and types of new corporations formed during last 3–5 years	Secretary of State's Office— Corporation Unit
Number and types of new start-ups	City and County records
Number and type of business permits issued	City and County records

Number and type of patents issued	U. S. Patent Office records
Level of participation in organizations (such as inventors' councils, trade associations, home-based business or entrepreneurs clubs or groups)	Survey of appropriate local organizations
Level of attendance at prebusiness workshops and business education courses	SBA, SCORE, SBDCs, Business Schools, Chambers of Commerce
Number of locally generated spin-off companies formed in last three years (number, type, parent firm)	Survey of major local corporations, Chamber members, banks, venture capitalists.

Extent of new business failures
(number and type)

City, County and/or State records,
Dun and Bradstreet

Number of start-up business plans
being considered by local banks,
503 companies, accounting firms,
attorneys and local venture
capitalists

Interviews and surveys

Worksheet Six: Analyzing the Local Economy— Commercial Real Estate Supply and Demand Assessment

Supply of Commercial Space

Number of sq. ft. of available space by rent level and by type of commercial property.

Type/Business	No. Sq. Ft.	Below market	Market rate	High rent
Retail				
Space				
Light Manuf.				
Industrial				
Warehouse				
Hi Tech Space i.e., R & D facility labs				

Length of average commercial lease offered by type of business activity.

Type of Business	Activity	No. Years
Retail		
Office space		
Light manuf.		
Industrial		
Warehouse		
R & D facility		

Demand for Commercial Space

Vacancy rate by type of commercial property

Type of Business	Vacancy Rate (%)
Retail	
Office space	
Light manufacturing	
Industrial	
Warehouse	
Hi tech space	

Number of business permits issued by type of business during last 12 months.

Type of Business	Number
Retail	
Wholesale	
Assembly	
Light manufacturing	
Industrial	
Hi tech R & D	
Professional services	

Survey and interview results. Ask respondents to rate on a continuum from low-high the level of demand in the community for various types of commercial space.

	Retail Space		
	Low	*Medium*	*High*
Commercial Realtors			
Bankers			
503 Companies			
Venture Capitalists			
City/County Officials			
Construction Firms			
Local Econ. Dev. Org.			
Chambers			

	Office Space		
	Low	Medium	High
Commercial Realtors			
Bankers			
503 Companies			
Venture Capitalists			
City/County Officials			
Construction Firms			
Local Econ. Dev. Org.			
Chambers			

	Light Manufacturing		
	Low	*Medium*	*High*
Commercial Realtors			
Bankers			
503 Companies			
Venture Capitalists			
City/County Officials			
Construction Firms			
Local Econ. Dev. Org.			
Chambers			

	Industrial Sites		
	Low	Medium	High
Commercial Realtors			
Bankers			
503 Companies			
Venture Capitalists			
City/County Officials			
Construction Firms			
Local Econ. Dev. Org.			
Chambers			

	Hi Tech R & D Facilities		
	Low	Medium	High
Commercial Realtors			
Bankers			
503 Companies			
Venture Capitalists			
City/County Officials			
Construction Firms			
Local Econ. Dev. Org.			
Chambers			

Worksheet Seven: Assessing the Small Business Support Network

Questions	*Sources*
Are classes on "Starting a New Business" available? By whom are they offered?	University, community colleges, SCORE, chamber, trade associations, existing businesses
Are there local programs providing technical assistance to small businesses? e.g., patent search and application, invention evaluation, business planning, overall management, marketing, accounting? If so, list below.	Same as above
Is there a local seed capital fund to assist businesses? Who administers it, source of funding, lending requirements?	Banks, venture capital new start-up 503 company, chamber city/county/state officials, SBA

Does the state have a small business loan program?	Same as above
Is there a service providing new businesses with information on available financial sources?	Same as above including university, community colleges, chamber
What are the general policies of local lending institutions toward small business lending, especially start-up business loans?	Same as above
Do local tax policies affect small business?	City/county officials, existing and new businesses

Does city or county have a one-stop business permit center? Are there problems/delays in getting necessary permits?	City/county officials, chamber, existing and new businesses
Does local media give adequate coverage to issues of concern to small businesses?	Same as above and local media persons
Does Chamber membership reflect a strong commitment to small business?	Existing and new businesses, local media, city/county officials, chamber

Worksheet Eight: Establish Community Goals and Objectives

Community Economic Development Goals

Process

1. The working groups should discuss and reach agreement on the community's overall economic goals.

   Example:
   > Promote Economic Growth
   > Diversify Local Economy
   > Revitalize Economically Deteriorated Area

2. Request all working group members to brainstorm a list of specific objectives which would measurably contribute toward reaching the community's goal(s). A partial list is provided below. Others may be suggested by members.

3. List all objectives submitted.

4. Prioritize the list.

5. Develop *Statement of Goals and Specific Objectives.*

Potential Objectives   Rank order

1. Job creation & retention   _____

2. Stimulate real estate development in specific areas   _____

3. Create marketing outlets for community products and services   _____

4. Tax base expansion   _____

5. Enhanced community's image as a center of productivity   _____

6. Fill gaps identified in local economy   _____

7. Create local investment opportunities in high-growth

8. Develop a high-tech or R & D business sector in the community   _____

9. Rehabilitate vacated commercial buildings   _____

10. Develop local suppliers for community's major companies _____

Worksheet Nine: Focus of Business Incubator

Organization of Management

1. For-profit ⎯⎯⎯⎯⎯
2. Non-profit ⎯⎯⎯⎯⎯

Type of Tenant Firms (Age of Business)

1. Start ups ⎯⎯⎯⎯⎯
2. Existing businesses ⎯⎯⎯⎯⎯
3. Mix (percentage) ⎯⎯⎯⎯⎯

Type of Tenant Firms (By industry classification)

1. Service ⎯⎯⎯⎯⎯
2. Light manufacturing ⎯⎯⎯⎯⎯
3. Research and development ⎯⎯⎯⎯⎯
4. Advanced technology ⎯⎯⎯⎯⎯
5. Retail ⎯⎯⎯⎯⎯
6. Involvement with import/export ⎯⎯⎯⎯⎯
7. Mix (percentage) ⎯⎯⎯⎯⎯
8. Other (specify) ⎯⎯⎯⎯⎯⎯⎯⎯⎯

Type of Tenant Firms (Targeted Population)

1. University Professors ⎯⎯⎯⎯⎯
2. Minorities ⎯⎯⎯⎯⎯
3. Women ⎯⎯⎯⎯⎯
4. Students ⎯⎯⎯⎯⎯
5. Spinoffs from major corporations ⎯⎯⎯⎯⎯
6. Other (specify) ⎯⎯⎯⎯⎯⎯⎯⎯⎯

Type of Facility

1. Former manufacturing plant ⎯⎯⎯⎯⎯
2. Abandoned school ⎯⎯⎯⎯⎯
3. Warehouse ⎯⎯⎯⎯⎯
4. Strip shopping center ⎯⎯⎯⎯⎯
5. Other (specify) ⎯⎯⎯⎯⎯⎯⎯⎯⎯

Location of Facility

1. Deteriorated or blighted neighborhood _____
2. Rural setting _____
3. Central business district _____
4. Science Park near university _____
5. Urban industrial area _____
6. Historic district _____

Worksheet Ten: Information on Incubator Facilities

1. Name of Facility _____

2. Owner of Facility _____

3. Basic Objectives _____

4. Management of Facility by _____

5. Date Opened _____

6. Size of Facility _____

7. Number of Tenants _____

8. Type of Tenants (by industry type)

_____

_____

9. Vacancy rate (%) _____

10. Number of Graduates _____

11. Location of Graduates _____

12. Type of Facility: New or Existing _____
    Method of Acquisition _____

13. Screening and Graduation Policies

_____

_____

14. Cost of Facility Acquisition and Renovation _____

15. Funding Sources _____

16. Major Operating Costs _____

_____

17. Major Operating Revenues (rent/square foot, fees, other)

_____

_____

18. Support Services Provided

Service	Supplier	Cost
_____	_____	_____
_____	_____	_____
_____	_____	_____

19. Financial Assistance to Tenant Firms

	By Whom?
Assistance	(Organization)
_____	_____
_____	_____
_____	_____

20. Management and Professional Services to Tenant Firms (what type of services, who provides)

Service	Supplier	Cost
_____	_____	_____
_____	_____	_____
_____	_____	_____

21. History of Incubator
    a. Reason for initiating project.
    b. Original working group: Representation.
    c. Major obstacles encountered. Solutions.
    d. Marketing strategy to identify tenants.
    e. Type of feasibility study done for project.

       Conducted by: _____

       Method: _____

    f. Community resources used.
    g. Continuing community response to project.

Worksheet Eleven: Facility Site Survey

Availability

Location	Land (for new building)		
	Cost	Est. Cost of Building	Advantages/Disadvantages

Location	Commercial Buildings		
	Cost	Est. Cost of Renovation	Advantages/Disadvantages

| | Publicly Owned Buildings | | |
Location	Cost	Est. Cost of Renovation	Advantages/Disadvantages

Evaluation

Site _____

Basic Requirements (of space, tenants)	*Good*	*Adequate*	*Inadequate*
_____	_____	_____	_____
_____	_____	_____	_____
_____	_____	_____	_____
_____	_____	_____	_____

Site _____

Basic Requirements (of space, tenants)	*Good*	*Adequate*	*Inadequate*
_____	_____	_____	_____
_____	_____	_____	_____
_____	_____	_____	_____
_____	_____	_____	_____

Site _____

Basic Requirements (of space, tenants)	*Good*	*Adequate*	*Inadequate*
_____	_____	_____	_____
_____	_____	_____	_____
_____	_____	_____	_____
_____	_____	_____	_____

Site _____

Basic Requirements (of space, tenants)	*Good*	*Adequate*	*Inadequate*
_____	_____	_____	_____
_____	_____	_____	_____
_____	_____	_____	_____
_____	_____	_____	_____

Worksheet Twelve: Management Plan

Organizational Structure

Management Purpose   For-profit _____   Non-profit _____

Decision Making Body   Existing board _____   New board _____
     Name of Organization _____

     Board Members: Number _____
           Representation: Duties:

           _____   _____

           _____   _____

           _____   _____

           Formal Board _____   Informal
Advisory Group   Arrangements _____

     Board Members   Number _____
     (if formal)   Representation: Duties:

           _____   _____

           _____   _____

           _____   _____

     Incubator Manager   Duties: Desired Qualification:

           _____   _____

           _____   _____

           _____   _____

     Basic Organizational Structure
         Decision-Making   Advisory
         Decision/Implementation
         Implementation

Operational Policies and Procedures

Services

Shared Service	Service	Provider (contracted/gov. program)
	_____	_____
	_____	_____
	_____	_____
	_____	_____

Available for Tenants	Service	Provider (contracted/gov. program)
	_____	_____
	_____	_____
	_____	_____

Financing (Operating expenses)	Amount needed	Methods	Responsibility
	_____	_____	_____
	_____	_____	_____
	_____	_____	_____

Tenant Policies
    Screening:
    Rental/Lease:
    Graduation:

Bibliography

"Academic 'Incubator' Concept Helps Hatch Young Entrepreneurs." *Christian Science Monitor,* 6 December 1983, 35.

Adams, Mescon, and Sheila Adams. "Incubating New Business Development: The Texas Connection." *Southwest Business and Economic Review,* August 1980, vol. 18, 1–12.

Advanced Technology Development: A Review of Small Business Incubator Initiatives. Harrisburg, Pa.: Governor's Office of Policy and Planning, 29 November 1982.

Allen, David N., Judith E. Ginsberg, and Susan A. Meiburger. *Home Grown Entrepreneurship: Pennsylvania's Small Business Incubators.* University Park: Pennsylvania State University, Institute of Public Administration, August 1984.

Appelbaum, Eileen. "High Tech and the Structural Employment of the 1980's" in *American Jobs and the Changing Industrial Base.* Cambridge, Mass.: Ballinger, 1984.

Armstrong, Jeanne, and John Mullin. *The Role of Planners in Fostering Industrial Growth from Within Their Local Communities.* New York: Association of Collegiate Schools of Planning, 19 October 1984.

Background Facts on the Akron-Summit Industrial Incubator Project. Akron, Ohio: Mayor's Office of Economic Development, 1981.

Bennett, Scott. "Hatchery." *Texas Business,* August 1984, 45.

Berger, Renee A. *The Small Business Incubator: Lessons Learned from Europe.* Washington, D.C.: Small Business Administration, Office of Private Sector Initiatives, 1984.

Birch, David L. "The Job Generation Process." *Birch Study.* Cambridge, Massachusetts: 1979.

Birch, David L., and Susan J. MacCracken. *The Role Played by High Technology Firms in Job Creation.* Cambridge: MIT Program on Neighborhood and Regional Change, 1984.

Brooks, Harvey, Lance Liebman, and Corrine S. Schelling, eds. *Public-Private Partnership: New Opportunities for Meeting Social Need.* Cambridge, Mass.: Ballinger, 1984.

Brooks, Jim. "High-Tech Incubators: Hatcheries or Hype?" *High-Tech Marketing* 2(April 1985).

Campbell, Candace. "Hatching Small Businesses." *Planning* 50(May 1984):19–24.

The Community and Small and Medium-sized Enterprises. Brussels: Commission of the European Communities, 1983.

Cooper, Arnold C. "The Entrepreneurship—Small Business Interface." In *Encyclopedia of Entrepreneurship.* Englewood, N.J.: Prentice-Hall, 1982.

Demuth, Jerry. "What Can Incubators Offer?" *Venture,* November 1984, 78–84.

Dorf, Richard C., and Barbara Purdy. *Incubators for Innovation—A Plan for California Regional Innovation and Job Creation.* Davis: University of California at Davis, 15 March 1985.

Douglas, Leon. "Small Business Incubator Meeting Set for Colorado Springs." *Nation's Cities Weekly,* 4 February 1985, vol. 8, 2.

"Enterprise: Ideas, Information and Inspiration to Help You Do Business a Better Way." *Working Woman,* July 1985, 31–34.

"The European Climate for Small Businesses—A Ten Country Study." *Economist Intelligence Unit, The Economist* London, 1983.

European Year of Small and Medium Enterprises, 1983: Report of the First Lancaster Conference, January, 1983. London: UK National Organising Committee, 1983.

"Facts about Small Business and the US Small Business Administration." Washington, D.C.: SBA Public Communications Division, February 1981.

"The Federal Laboratories: Technology Resources and Transfer Champions." Paper presented to the symposium Leaping the Technology Transfer Barriers, American Chemical Society, 28 August 1984.

Gibb, J.M., ed. *Science Parks and Innovation Centers: Their Economic and Social Impact.* New York: Elsevier Science, 1985.

Gibson, Thomas G. "How Early Is 'Early Stage'?" *Venture,* March 1984, vol. 6, 120–22.

Gissy, Francine, "Incubator Industrial Buildings: A Case Study." *Economic Development Review,* vol. 2, 48–52.

Healy, Tim. "Incubators Aim to Hatch New Firms." *Puget Sound Business Journal,* 4 March 1985, 1.

Hoad, William M., and Peter Rosko. *Management Factors Contributing to the Success and Failure of New Small Manufacturers.* Ann Arbor: University of Michigan, Bureau of Business Research, 1974.

Imai, Ken'ichi. "Japan's Industrial Society: Technical Innovation and Formation of a Network Society." *Journal of Japanese Trade and Industry,* 1983, no. 4, 43–48.

Incubators for Small Business. Washington, D.C.: Small Business Administration, Office of Private Sector Initiatives, June 1984.

"Incubators Hatch More Than Chickens." *High Technology,* September 1984, 70–71.

Innovation in Small and Medium Firms. Paris: Organization for Economic Cooperation and Development, 1982.

Karlin, Beth. "Britain's Agencies For High Technology Try New Approach." *Wall Street Journal.* 21 October 1983.

Lavelle, June. *The Industrial Council of Northwest Chicago—Update.* Chicago: Industrial Council of Northwest Chicago, 1985.

McGarvey, Alan. "GLEB's Job-Creation Efforts Begin to Show Results." *Municipal Review and AMA News* (London), 1984.

More Can Be Done to Ensure That Industrial Parks Create More Jobs. Washington, D.C.: Government Printing Office, 1980.

Morse, Richard, and John O. Flender. "The Role of New Technical Enterprises in the US Economy." Technical Advisory Board, US Department of Commerce. Washington, D.C.: Government Printing Office, 1976.

National Council For Urban Economic Development. *Akron-Summit Industrial Incubator, Akron (Ohio).* Washington, D.C.: NCUED Clearinghouse, 1984.

———. *Broome County (N.Y.) Industrial Incubator.* Washington, D.C.: NCUED Clearinghouse, 1984.

———. *Genesis Development Center, Wichita (Kan.).* Washington, D.C.: NCUED Clearinghouse, 1984.

———. Fulton-Carroll Center, Chicago." Washington, D.C.: NCUED Clearinghouse, 1984.

———. *"High-Tech" and University Affiliated Incubators.* Washington, D.C. NCUED Clearinghouse, 1984.

———. *Incubators: Adaptive Reuse and Industrial Rehabs.* Washington, D.C.: NCUED Clearinghouse, 1984.

———. *Incubators: Newly Constructed Facilities and Facilities Keyed to Industrial Parks.* Washington, D.C.: NCUED Clearinghouse, 1984.

———. *The J.B. Blood Building, Lynn (Mass.).* Washington, D.C.: NCUED Clearinghouse, 1984.

———. *Metropolitan Center for High Technology, Detroit.* Washington, D.C.: NCUED Clearinghouse, 1984.

———. *Model Documents: Tenant Application Forms and Lease Agreements.* Washington, D.C.: NCUED Clearinghouse, 1984.

———. *St. Paul's Small Business Incubator Facility.* Washington, D.C.: NCUED Clearinghouse, 1984.

———. *University City Science Center, Philadelphia.* Washington, D.C.: NCUED Clearinghouse, 1984.

Nelton, Sharon. "Incubators For Baby Businesses." *Nation's Business,* November 1984, 40–41.

Network. Philadelphia: The North East Tier Ben Franklin Advanced Technology Center, 1985, Vol. 1, No. 2 (Newsletter).

Nomura, Tatsuo. "The Competitive Edge of Medium-Sized Firms." *Economic Eye,* March 1983.

Phalon, Richard. "University as Venture Capitalist." *Forbes,* 19 December 1983, vol. 132, 82–93.

Plosila, Walter, and David N. Allen. *Small Business Incubators and Public Policy: Implications for State and Local Development Strategies.* Philadelphia: Pennsylvania Department of Commerce, December 1984.

The Promotion of Small Business: A 7-Country Study, 2 vols. London: Economists Advisory Group, 1980.

"Pueblo: 'Incubator' Gives New Companies a Head Start." *Colorado Business,* August 1984, vol. 11, 62.

Purcell, Mia. "The Industrial Incubator." Information Service Report No. 27. Washington, D.C.: National Council for Urban Economic Development, February 1984.

Reich, Robert B. "High-Tech Industrial Policy: Comparing the United States with Other Advanced Nations." *Journal of Japanese Trade and Industry.* 1983, no. 4, 31–33.

Santana, Ruth. "Small Business Incubators to Be Studied at Workshop." *Nation's Cities Weekly,* 19 November 1984, vol. 7, 24.

Shapero, Albert. "Entrepreneurship Key to Self Renewing Economics." *Commentary,* April 1981, vol. 5.

Small Business Incubator Sample Information Package. Washington, D.C.: Small Business Administration, Office of Private Sector Initiatives, 1984.

Smilor, Raymond, and Michael Gill, eds. *New Business Incubators.* Austin: The University of Texas at Austin, IC^2 Institute, 1984. (Papers from a workshop on new business incubators, Los Alamos, New Mexico, April 2–3, 1984.)

Smilor, Raymond and Michael Gill eds. "New Business Incubators Data Book." Austin: The University of Texas at Austin, IC^2 Institute, 1984. (Prepared for conference on small business incubators, "Technology and New Business Growth," San Antonio, November 29–December 1, 1984.)

"Special Report: Growth In Business Incubators Seen Helping Some Areas Create Jobs: Here's How." *Economic & Industrial Development News,* 19 December 1983.

"Special Report—Universities Emerge As an Important Catalyst in the New Business Development Process." *Venture Capital Journal,* August 1983, 7.

Starting A Small Business Incubator: A Handbook for Sponsors and Developers. Washington, D.C.: Illinois Department of Commerce & Community Affairs and the U.S. Small Business Administration, Region V, Office of Private Sector Initiatives, August 1984.

State Activities in Venture Capital, Early-Stage Financing, and Secondary Markets. Washington, D.C.: Small Business Administration, Office of Advocacy, May 1984.

The State of Small Business: A Report of the President. Washington, D.C.: Government Printing Office, March 1984.

The States and Small Business: Programs and Activities. Washington, D.C.: Small Business Administration, Office of Advocacy, October 1983. (State-by-state summary of programs and assistance available for small business.)

A Summary of Major State and Local Small Business Issues in 1984. Washington, D.C.: Small Business Administration, Office of Advocacy, March 1984.

Summary of the Economic Impact of the Small Business Investment Company Program (Deloitte Haskins and Sells and Arthur D. Little, eds.). Washington, D.C.: National Association of Small Business Investment Companies, 1982.

"Technology, Innovation & Regional Economic Development, Background Paper #2." OTA-BP-STI-25. Washington, D.C.: U.S. Congress, Office of Technology Assessment, February 1984.

Technopolises: Now in Japan. Tokyo: Japanese External Trade Organization, 1983.

Temali, Mihailo, and Candace Campbell. *Business Incubator Profiles: A National Survey.* Minneapolis: University of Minnesota, Hubert Humphrey Institute of Public Affairs, 1984.

Thorne, John R., and John G. Ball. "Entrepreneurs and Their Companies." Karl H.

Vesper, ed., *Frontiers of Entrepreneurship Research.* Wellesley, Mass.: Babson College, 1981, pp. 65–83.

Tietz, Michael. *Small Business & Employment Growth in California.* Berkeley: Institute of University of California, Institute of Urban and Regional Development, 1981.

Vaughan, Roger J. *Small and New Business Development: An Action Guide for State Government.* Coalition of Northeast Governors, Policy Research Center, 1983.

Verduin, Paul H., and James S. Roberts. *Small Business Incubation—Successful Models from Abroad.* Learning from Abroad Series No. 7. Washington, D.C.: Council for International Urban Liaison, 1984.

Vesper, Karl. *Entrepreneurship and National Policy.* Chicago: Walter Heller International Institute for Small Business Policy Papers, 1983.

"Workers in Transition—Communities Struggle to Provide Help Anonymously." *Industry Week,* 1 April 1985, vol. 225, 35–42.

Index

About the Authors

Raymond W. Smilor is the associate director of the IC^2 Institute and a member of the faculty in the Department of Marketing in the College of Business Administration, The University of Texas at Austin. He holds the Judson Neff Centennial Fellowship in the IC^2 Institute. He is also the director and editor-in-chief of the *International Journal of High Technology Marketing.*

Dr. Smilor has served as a research fellow for a National Science Foundation international exchange program on computers and management between the United States and the Soviet Union and has been a leading participant in the planning and organization of many regional, national, and international conferences, symposia, and workshops.

He serves as a consultant to business, government, and the nonprofit sector, and he is chairman of HighMark International, Inc., a market strategy and research firm.

Dr. Smilor's academic works cover a wide variety of interdisciplinary subjects. He has taught courses in management at the graduate and the undergraduate level and currently teaches a course on marketing, technology, and entrepreneurship. His research interests include science and technology transfer, entrepreneurship, marketing strategies for high-technology products, and creative and innovative management techniques. He earned his Ph.D. in U.S. history at The University of Texas at Austin. He is co-editor of *Corporate Creativity: Robust Companies and the Entrepreneurial Spirit* (Praeger, 1984), *Improving U.S. Energy Security* (Ballinger, 1985), *Managing Take-Off in Fast Growth Companies* (Praeger 1986), and *The Art and Science of Entrepreneurship* (Ballinger, 1986); and co-author of *Financing and Managing Fast-Growth Companies: The Venture Capital Process* (Lexington Books, 1985).

Michael Doud Gill, Jr., is an associate with United Capital Ventures, Inc., and a research fellow at the IC^2 Institute, The University of Texas at Austin. He has been an active researcher and writer on the venture capital industry for the past two years and is co-author of *Financing and Managing Fast-Growth Companies: The Venture Capital Process* (Lexington Books, 1985) and *Technology Venturing Databook: Making and Securing the Future* (IC^2 Institute, The University of Texas at Austin, May 1985).

Mr. Gill has published a number of articles on venture capital through the IC^2 Institute and has been invited to speak on the subject to various groups. His research interests include technology commercialization, regional economic development, venture capital, new business incubators, high-technology employment and financing, and investment in public issues of new technology stocks. He holds a B.A. in both economics and history from Villanova University and an M.B.A. from The University of Texas at Austin.

About the Sponsors

The following organizations sponsored the national survey on new business incubators.

IC² Institute

The IC² Institute at The University of Texas at Austin is a major research center for the study of innovation, creativity, and capital (hence IC²). The institute studies and analyzes information about the enterprise system through an integrated program of research, conferences, and publications.

IC² studies provide frameworks for dealing with current and critical unstructured problems from a private sector point of view. The key areas of research and study concentration of IC² include the management of technology; creative and innovative management; measuring the state of society; dynamic business development and entrepreneurship; econometrics, economic analysis and management sciences; and the evaluation of attitudes, opinions, and concerns on key issues.

The institute generates a strong interaction between scholarly developments and real-world issues by conducting national and international conferences, developing initiatives for private and public sector consideration, assisting in the establishment of professional organizations and other research institutes and centers, and maintaining collaborative efforts with universities, communities, states, and government agencies.

IC² research is published through monographs, policy papers, technical working papers, research articles, and three major series of books.

Office of Private Sector Initiatives, U.S. Small Business Administration

The U.S. Small Business Administration's Office of Private Sector Initiatives (OPSI) was created in 1982. It seeks to develop promising public/private partnerships that foster small business development and growth and that combine the unique resources and skills of government and the private sector.

The OPSI is an innovative arm of the Small Business Administration, watching new trends in economic and business development and creating opportunities to test-market new business development tools. It is concerned principally with training, education, information, and model developments. The OPSI seeks to reach out to new small business markets, economic development professionals, and private organizations that understand that a thriving small business community can mean substantial returns to local and national economies.

Peat, Marwick, Mitchell & Co.

Peat, Marwick is one of the largest professional service organizations in the world, with more than 30,000 personnel and 300 offices. It provides auditing and accounting, tax, management consulting, and private business advisory services. Peat, Marwick's sponsorship of the incubator survey and this book was through three of its practice areas.

Education and Other Institutions Practice

The firm's Education and Other Institutions Practice provides a wide range of services to colleges and universities, research centers, and other organizations. Services include assistance with establishing effective technology transfer programs, incubator facilities, and creative financing approaches.

Private Business Advisory Services (PBAS) Practice

The firm's PBAS Practice focuses on privately owned and growing businesses. Professionals in this practice are specially trained and experienced to assist in the startup and early growth stages of companies—helping to prepare business plans, locate financing, and establish initial systems and controls, and assisting in many other areas that are important to the success of new businesses.

High-Technology Practice

Peat, Marwick's High-Technology Practice provides specialized services to high-technology companies of all sizes and at all stages of development. Assistance to entrepreneurs and early-stage companies is provided through the combined resources of the High-Technology and PBAS Practices. In addition, the firm's high-technology professionals actively assist states and local communities in building or improving their high-technology environments.

DATE DUE

JAN 1 0 1987			
DEC 1 1987			
JUL 0 2 1993			
DEC 0 7 1993			
DEC 0 2 1994			